Ordnance Survey

SNOWDONIA

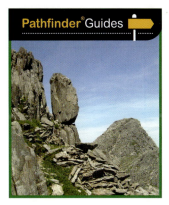

Pathfinder®Guides

Outstanding Circular Walks

Compiled by
Terry Marsh

Contents

At-a-glance

Walk		Page	🏁		📷 SH	🪧	⛰️	🕐
1	Aber Falls	10	Bont Newydd, Aber	SH 662720	3 miles (4.5km)	670ft (205m)	1½ hrs
2	Cwm Pennant	12	North of Llanfihangel-y-pennant	SH 532476	3¼ miles (5.1km)	490ft (150m)	2 hrs
3	Precipice Walk	14	North of Dolgellau	SH 745211	3½ miles (5.5km)	705ft (215m)	2 hrs
4	Ceunant Cynfal	16	Bont Newydd	SH 712408	3¾ miles (6km)	755ft (230m)	2 hrs
5	Tal-y-llyn Lake (Llyn Mwyngil)	18	Tal-y-llyn	SH 714095	4 miles (6.3km)	625ft (190m)	2 hrs
6	Capel Curig	20	Capel Curig	SH 720582	4 miles (6.4km)	655ft (200m)	2½ hrs
7	Penmaenpool and the Mawddach Trail	22	Penmaenpool	SH 695185	5 miles (8km)	790ft (240m)	2½ hrs
8	Llyn y Gader and Beddgelert Forest	24	Rhyd Ddu	SH 571525	5 miles (8km)	870ft (265m)	2½ hrs
9	Lledr valley	28	Dolwyddelan	SH 737521	6 miles (9.4km)	1,115ft (340m)	3 hrs
10	Gwydyr Forest and Trefriw	31	Llanrwst	SH 798616	6¼ miles (9.9km)	870ft (265m)	3 hrs
11	Coed-y-brenin	34	Ganllwyd	SH 726243	5¼ miles (8.3km)	755ft (230m)	3 hrs
12	Vale of Ffestiniog	37	Rhŷd-y-sarn	SH 690422	5¾ miles (9km)	900ft (275m)	3 hrs
13	Cregennen Lakes (Llynnau Cregennen)	40	Arthog	SH 640148	5½ miles (8.6km)	1,100ft (335m)	3½ hrs
14	Tanygrisiau and Rhosydd	44	Tanygrisiau	SH 683452	5½ miles (8.6km)	1,380ft (420m)	3½ hrs
15	Tryfan	48	Ogwen valley	SH 659602	3 miles (4.8km)	1,755ft (535m)	3½ hrs
16	Moel Hebog	51	Beddgelert	SH 590481	4¾ miles (7.4km)	2,480ft (755m)	3½ hrs
17	Drum and Llyn Anafon	54	Aber (Upper car park)	SH 675716	6¾ miles (10.7km)	2,000ft (610m)	4 hrs
18	Pont Scethin	58	Dyffryn Ardudwy	SH 586232	8 miles (12.6km)	1,295ft (395m)	4½ hrs
19	Cnicht	61	Croesor	SH 631446	6¾ miles (10.7km)	1,950ft (595m)	4½ hrs
20	Carnedd Llywelyn	64	Ogwen valley, Gwern Gof Isaf farm	SH 685602	6½ miles (10.5km)	2,540ft (775m)	4½ hrs
21	Gwydyr Forest and the Swallow Falls	67	Betws-y-coed	SH 795565	8½ miles (13.5km)	1,625ft (495m)	5 hrs
22	Nanmor valley and Aberglaslyn	70	Beddgelert	SH 590481	8½ miles (13.3km)	1,770ft (540m)	5 hrs
23	Aran Benllyn	74	Pont y Pandy, Llanuwchllyn	SH 879297	7½ miles (12km)	2,295ft (700m)	5 hrs
24	Moel Eilio	77	Llanberis	SH 580601	8 miles (13km)	2,445ft (745m)	5 hrs
25	Snowdon (Yr Wyddfa)	80	Pen-y-pass	SH 647556	7¼ miles (11.7km)	2,920ft (890m)	5 hrs
26	Cadair Idris	84	Minffordd	SH 732115	6 miles (9.5km)	3,020ft (920m)	5 hrs
27	Glyder Fach and Glyder Fawr	86	Ogwen	SH 649604	5¼ miles (8.5km)	2,770ft (845m)	5 hrs
28	Y Llethr and Moelfre	89	Tal-y-bont, Dyffryn Ardudwy	SH 589218	11¾ miles (18.8km)	2,840ft (865m)	6½ hrs

Comments

An easy walk through a beautiful wooded valley leading to the stunning display of Aber Falls, almost an icon of North Wales, and hugely popular as a result.

A walk in remote and lonely country in the upper reaches of the Dwyfor, surrounded by impressive mountain ranges on all sides.

A short walk that gives a succession of views over mountain, forest and estuary, finishing with a delightful stroll beside a small reservoir.

Most of this walk is through a beautifully wooded ravine above the Ceunant Cynfal, with delightful views down the Vale of Ffestiniog that include the bulky Moelwyn Mawr.

On the pleasant circuit of Tal-y-llyn Lake, you enjoy superb and ever-changing views across the lake to the surrounding mountains.

Making a wide circle around the spread-out village of Capel Curig, this walk takes in delightful woodland and riverside paths, while affording excellent views of Moel Siabod and the Snowdon Horseshoe.

There are fine views of Cadair Idris and the Mawddach Estuary from this delightful and undemanding walk, which concludes with an agreeable amble along the course of an old railway.

This walk around Llyn y Gadar offers the prospect of fine mountain scenery, from the Snowdon massif on the one hand, and the Nantlle Ridge and Moel Hebog on the other; all very inspiring.

A walk of much delight, starting through pleasant woodland, before descending to accompany the River Lledr in its gorge; splendid views across the valley to more distant Snowdonia summits.

A varied and attractive walk that combines a lovely stroll beside the River Conwy with an amble along the edge of Gwydyr forest, and a visit to an ancient and interesting settlement.

Two outstanding waterfalls are the main features of this easy walk through the confines of Coed-y-brenin, wherein gold has been found in the recent past.

An opportunity to explore the beautiful wooded confines of the Vale of Ffestiniog and a couple of National Nature Reserves.

Beginning with an ascent through ancient broad-leaved woodland into a theatre of considerable history and prehistory, providing excellent views northwards across the Mawddach Estuary to the hills of Welsh gold.

A walk through a landscape of industrial history, both inspirational and melancholic. The harsh reminder of men's industry is set against the rugged beauty of encircling mountains of grace and elegance.

Not for the faint-hearted, this ascent of Tryfan's north ridge is a Snowdonian classic. Rockwork and complex route finding throughout most of the walk, although there is a splendid opportunity for relaxation at the end.

A steep and energetic ascent to a popular Victorian highlight, a splendid panoramic viewpoint above the valley town of Beddgelert.

A relatively gentle ascent to the eastern end of the Carneddau, through a prehistoric landscape. One short steep descent, but otherwise good tracks and paths are the order of the day.

A splendid jaunt into the inspiringly beautiful reaches of the Afon Ysgethin; the walking is easy throughout, and affords lovely views of Barmouth Bay and the southern Rhinog summits.

A straightforward but ultimately steep climb to the distinctive summit of Cnicht, followed by a fine ridge walk, and a visit to an abandoned slate mine.

Climb to the highest summit of the Carneddau range, named after the last native Prince of Wales. There are splendid views across the Ogwen valley to Tryfan and the Glyders, and into the upper reaches of Cwm Eigiau.

After an initial climb through the conifers of the Gwydyr Forest to a viewpoint, the remainder of the walk is through the thickly wooded gorge of the Afon Llugwy, passing the celebrated Swallow Falls.

A not overly difficult walk through an inspirational landscape, and concluding with a fascinating trek through the Aberglaslyn Pass; especially delightful in late summer and early autumn when the heather is in bloom.

A splendid romp to a much-loved mountain top, with a fabulous panorama that embraces virtually the whole of the National Park. Agreeable undulations and a guiding fence take you ever upwards to the quartzy summit.

A special and mainly grassy romp over soft-moulded hills above Llanberis, that bring the reward of solitude and leg-swinging freedom in return for such effort as is involved.

The ultimate ambition of all serious walkers visiting North Wales, a tremendously satisfying outing, rugged all the way and with magnificent views throughout.

The ascent of Cadair Idris from Minffordd is energetic and demanding, but the scenery illustrates why this is one of the most popular walks in Snowdonia.

A rugged and challenging walk, to be attempted only by strong walkers in good weather. There is rock scrambling involved, and the descent of a steep scree slope; altogether invigorating, but not for the timid.

A long and delightful walk along a mainly straightforward route to the highest summit of the Rhinogs. The chance to embrace an outlying summit of ancient significance should not be missed.

Keymap

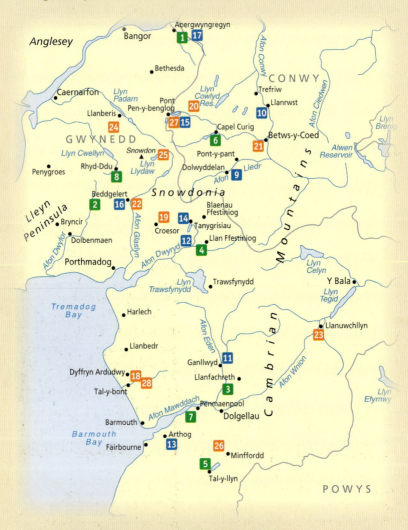

Introduction to Snowdonia

Soon after passing through Colwyn Bay, driving westwards, you enter the ancient Welsh kingdom of Gwynedd, and shortly arrive at the Conwy Estuary, the eastern frontier of what we call Snowdonia. In the Middle Ages, Gwynedd was the last stronghold of Welsh independence; today it is the foremost bastion of Welsh language and culture, along with the island of Anglesey to the north and the Lleyn Peninsula to the west.

From whichever direction you approach, the mountains of Snowdonia present a magnificent spectacle – row upon row of high ridges and formidable peaks. Presiding over this array is Yr Wyddfa, the highest peak in Britain south of Scotland. It is known by its more familiar name, allegedly bestowed upon it by Dark Age sailors, who when voyaging from Ireland to Wales saw snow-covered hills on the skyline and christened them the Snowy Hills, or 'Snaudune', initially a collective name that later became restricted to the highest peak only.

The Snowdonia mountains can be divided into a number of clearly defined ranges, each with their own characteristics. By far the most popular and most frequently climbed are the Carneddau, Glyders and Snowdon itself. The great ridges and sweeping grassy slopes of the Carneddau cover an extensive area between the Conwy valley and Nant Ffrancon, and in the north descend abruptly to the coast. Between Nant Ffrancon and the Llanberis pass rise the Glyders, their shattered volcanic rocks providing the spectacular pinnacles and formations that litter the summits of Glyder Fawr and Glyder Fach. Beyond Llanberis Pass is Snowdon, its summit accessible by an easy train ride as well as a harder but infinitely more satisfying walk, and to the west of Snowdon the Hebog range, Mynydd Mawr and the Nantlle Ridge, collectively known as the Eifionydd Hills, form the western face of the mountains.

The central zone of Snowdonia comprises the shapely mass of Moel Siabod between the Llugwy and Lledr valleys, the Moelwyns and Cnicht, the latter nicknamed the 'Welsh Matterhorn' because of its instantly recognisable pointed appearance when seen from the west. Also in the central area are the isolated twin Arenig peaks, whose outlines can be seen across the featureless expanses of the Migneint.

On the other side of Bala Lake, the Arans comprises a long ridge running south-westwards towards the Rhinogs and Cadair Idris, which lie close to the Cardigan Bay coast. The Rhinogs stretch in a long line from the Vale of Ffestiniog in the north to the Mawddach Estuary in the south. Their bare and hard Cambrian rocks, part of a massive upthrust known by geologists as the Harlech Dome, provide some of the roughest and most remote walking in the whole of the region. To the south of the Mawddach towers the familiar profile of Cadair Idris, not the highest mountain in southern Snowdonia but undoubtedly the best-loved and most popular in Wales south of the Carneddau-Glyders-Snowdon group.

There is more to Snowdonia, however, than mountains. The region has plenty of

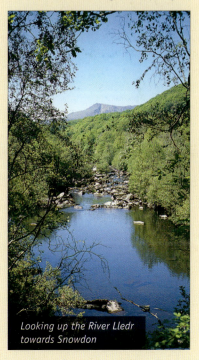

Looking up the River Lledr towards Snowdon

easy, low-level walks as well. Separating the ranges are delightful valleys: some, like the gorges of the Llugwy and Lledr near Betws-y-coed or the almost perpendicular Aberglaslyn Pass, are narrow and steep-sided; others, such as the Dysynni valley below Cadair Idris and the well-wooded Vale of Ffestiniog, are more green and open. Scattered throughout the area are a large number of lakes of varying sizes set amidst varying terrain: small lakes like Llyn Idwal and Llyn Cau hemmed in by steep and rocky slopes; larger mountain lakes

Water chute near Llyn y Gader

like the exceptionally beautiful Llyn Gwynant, Llyn Cwm Bychan, Tal-y-Ilyn, and Bala Lake (Llyn Tegid), the largest natural lake in Wales, situated in more gentle country.

The castles of Snowdonia

When travelling through Snowdonia, the foremost historic remains that catch the eye are the great medieval castles. But there are impressive prehistoric monuments, too, although Roman remains are scanty and the relative poverty of the area means that it is not rich in either ecclesiastical buildings – medieval churches are invariably small and plain though there are some gems – or in large country houses.

The castles, however, are among the finest in Europe. Secure within the natural defences of their mountain fortress and with guaranteed food supplies from Anglesey, the princes of Gwynedd became the most powerful of the native Welsh rulers, and in the early 13th century, Llywelyn the Great probably came nearer to creating a united and independent Welsh nation than anyone. Imitating the English kings and barons, these princes erected strong and impressive castles in the late 12th and early 13th centuries, and there are substantial remains of these at Dolbadarn, Dolwyddelan (reputed birthplace of Llywelyn the Great), Criccieth (later rebuilt by the English) and the highly atmospheric Castell y Bere.

Llywelyn the Great's death in 1240 was followed by civil wars, and in 1272 the accession to the English throne of Edward I, a man determined to extend his authority over all parts of Britain,

spelt the end of Welsh independence. Gwynedd was invaded, Llywelyn ap Gruffydd (last native prince of Wales) and his brother were killed and Welsh resistance was crushed. In order to consolidate his conquest Edward I encircled Snowdonia with the formidable and highly expensive castles of Conwy, Beaumaris, Caernarfon and Harlech, all embodying the latest sophistications of castle construction and all built near the coast to allow for easy transport of supplies and reinforcements in case of rebellion. But there were few rebellions, apart from Owain Glyndwr's last brave attempt to forge an independent Wales in the early 15th century, and these castles remain as examples of medieval military architecture at its most advanced and refined.

Quarrying and tourism

The most striking and large-scale man-made intrusions on the landscape of Snowdonia come from 19th- and 20th-century industrial and commercial developments. Victorian urban expansion created a huge demand for roofing slates, most of which were supplied by the slate quarries of Snowdonia, especially those around Blaenau Ffestiniog, Llanberis and Bethesda. Great scars appeared on the mountainsides, new settlements rapidly expanded to house the workers, and railways were built to transport the slate from the mines down to the ports at Port Dinorwic, Porthmadog and Twywn. The industry reached its peak at the end of the 19th century and subsequently suffered a rapid decline; now only a handful of quarries survive. But although no one can pretend that these quarries with their waste tips and attendant buildings enhance the landscape, or that the Victorian quarrying villages are picturesque, the remains of this derelict industry and the railways that once served it have become major tourist attractions.

It was around the time that slate-quarrying was starting to develop that the first tourists were beginning to 'discover' Snowdonia. These were the Romantics – artists, writers and intellectuals who were thrilled by the savage and untamed beauty of the region. Betws-y-coed was a particularly popular area for them because of its picturesque location at the meeting of three valleys, its steep wooded hillsides, the proximity of the Swallow Falls and the thickly wooded ravine of the Conwy on which they bestowed the suitably romantic name of the Fairy Glen.

Later the railways brought many more visitors into the region – holidaymakers to the coastal resorts of Llandudno, Barmouth and Aberdovey, and walkers and climbers into the mountains. Of all the recreational opportunities available in Snowdonia, walking and rock-climbing have always been paramount and many

Alpine enthusiasts and Himalayan adventurers first 'cut their teeth' on Crib Goch, Tryfan or Cadair Idris.

Tourism has continued to expand to become a vital part of the region's economy, but other 20th-century commercial pressures have had a more significant impact on the landscape: the extensive conifer plantations of Gwydyr, Beddgelert, Coed y Brenin and Dyfi forests, the construction of reservoirs, especially in the valleys of the eastern Carneddau, and the building of the nuclear power station at Trawsfynydd.

In 1951 Snowdonia became a National Park, the second largest of the 13 National Parks of England and Wales. Within this area there are opportunities for walks to suit every conceivable taste, age range and degree of fitness – challenging and strenuous mountain walks, gentle strolls by rivers and lakes, pleasant woodland rambles and invigorating coastal walks. But wherever you roam the eye is inevitably drawn to those noble mountain ranges that fill the horizon – the Snowy Hills or 'Snaudune' of the early seafarers.

This book includes a list of waypoints alongside the description of the walk, so that you can enjoy the full benefits of gps should you wish to. For more information on using your gps, read the Pathfinder® Guide *GPS for Walkers*, by gps teacher and navigation trainer, Clive Thomas (ISBN 978-0-7117-4445-5). For essential information on map reading and basic navigation, read the Pathfinder® Guide *Map Reading Skills* by the author of this guide, Terry Marsh (ISBN 978-0-7117-4978-8). Both titles are available in bookshops or can be ordered online at www.pathfinderwalks.co.uk

Aber Falls

Aber Falls

Start
Bont Newydd, Aber

Distance
3 miles (4.5km)

Height gain
670 feet (205m)

Approximate time
1½ hours

Route terrain
Broad tracks; woodland

P Parking
Roadside parking areas beside Bont Newydd, ¾ mile south-east of Abergwyngregyn. If these are full, cross the bridge and turn right to find the upper car park (Pay and Display)

OS maps
Landranger 115 (Snowdon/Yr Wyddfa), Explorer OL17 (Snowdon/Yr Wyddfa)

GPS waypoints
SH 662 720
Ⓐ SH 663 718
Ⓑ SH 668 700
Ⓒ SH 669 704

There can be few short walks more agreeable than this – a gentle stroll through a beautifully wooded and steep-sided valley on the northern fringes of Snowdonia to the spectacular Aber Falls. The return leg brings glimpses of the Menai Strait and beyond that, Anglesey.

Start by taking the gate beside Bont Newydd and walking upstream into Coedydd Aber National Nature Reserve, with the Afon Rhaeadr-fawr on your left. Cross a footbridge and go ahead to and through a gate to gain a gravelled track Ⓐ. Turn right along this.

This track rises easily and gradually: keep following the main trail through open woodland and meadow – wood pasture –

The spectacular Aber Falls

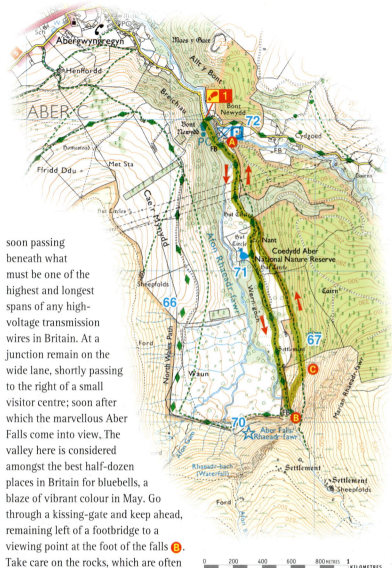

soon passing beneath what must be one of the highest and longest spans of any high-voltage transmission wires in Britain. At a junction remain on the wide lane, shortly passing to the right of a small visitor centre; soon after which the marvellous Aber Falls come into view. The valley here is considered amongst the best half-dozen places in Britain for bluebells, a blaze of vibrant colour in May. Go through a kissing-gate and keep ahead, remaining left of a footbridge to a viewing point at the foot of the falls **B**. Take care on the rocks, which are often slippery.

Return to the kissing-gate, but do not use it. Instead, turn right to use the ladder-stile into the fringe of the National Trust's vast Carneddau Estate. Head towards a conifer plantation edge on a rough, rising path through a boulder field to a ladder-stile into the plantation **C**.

Take the wider and lower of the two paths, meandering gently through the trees to another ladder-stile. From here go ahead on a wood-side path, gradually dropping to meet the outward route on the wide gravelled track well below the visitor centre. Turn right to retrace this back to Bont Newydd. As you reach the gate giving on to the bridge spanning the Afon Rhaeadr-fawr, keep right, through a car park and walk out to join the valley road at Bont Newydd ●

Start

Gated bridge over the Afon Dwyfor, 2 miles north of the church at Llanfihangel-y-pennant, which is signed off the A487 at Dolbenmaen

Distance

3¼ miles (5.1km)

Height gain

490 feet (150m)

Approximate time

2 hours

Route terrain

Mainly farmland paths and tracks

Parking

Roadside verges just before gated bridge

OS maps

Landranger 115 (Snowdon/Yr Wyddfa), Explorer OL17 (Snowdon/Yr Wyddfa)

GPS waypoints

🔲 SH 532 476
Ⓐ SH 533 479
Ⓑ SH 543 487
Ⓒ SH 546 492
Ⓓ SH 540 492

Cwm Pennant

The wild, remote beauty of Cwm Pennant, the upper reaches of the Afon Dwyfor, so inspired the Welsh shepherd-poet Eifion Wyn that he is supposed to have said as he lay dying: 'Oh God, why didst Thou make Cwm Pennant so beautiful and the life of an old shepherd so short?' This walk certainly reveals the beauty of the valley, cradled by lonely and impressive mountains on three sides – the Hebog range to the east and Nantlle ridge to the north and west and linked to the 'outside world' by just one narrow, winding lane. Part of the route follows the track of a disused tram road which leads to the remains of quarry buildings, an indication that even this seemingly isolated, untouched and unspoilt area, on the western fringes of Snowdonia, was not immune from Victorian industrial exploitation.

🔲 Cross the bridge over the Afon Dwyfor and walk along the lane to where it bears left to recross the river Ⓐ. Here keep ahead on a rough track leading to a farm. Enter the farmyard and use the waymarked gate to the right of a barn. Walk through to a junction and turn left (waymarked as a bridleway); shortly, fork right onto a narrower, waymarked path.

In 200yds, go through a bridle-gate, cross a stream and keep ahead on a faint path across the rough pasture and below gorse bushes. Cross a boggy area and keep ahead to a waymark post where you turn sharp right on an obvious path, zigzagging up to a third waymark post. From here, look half-left for another bridle-gate. Take this and head slightly left uphill to pass by a fence corner, then rise more steeply to find the grassy track bed of an old tram road Ⓑ.

Bear left along this, the line of the Gorseddau tram road which linked slate quarries and a small iron mine to Porthmadog from the 1830s until it closed in 1882. Enjoy sweeping views of the impressive head of Cwm Dwyfor from this easy, level path, eventually reaching two bridle-gates either side of a stream Ⓒ.

Turn left to the ruined quarry buildings. Pass immediately right of them and pick up an obvious path around the snout of a crag to the left of the cutting. Walk this to a ladder-stile on your left near a ruined cottage. Climb this and look for the path that descends in front of the ruins and is waymarked by yellow discs on posts. At the second yellow disc, turn half-left, heading

Old quarry buildings in Cwm Pennant

directly in line for the tarred lane on the valley floor. Further posts guide you down to the Afon Dwyfor at an old ford and adjacent ladder-stile **D**.

Join the tarred lane here and remain on it past the farm and through to a bridge at **A**. Cross the bridge and turn right to return to the parking area at the gated bridge. ●

SCALE 1:25 000 or 2½ INCHES TO 1 MILE 4CM to 1KM

Precipice Walk

Start

North of Dolgellau

Distance

3½ miles (5.5km)

Height gain

705 feet (215m)

Approximate time

2 hours

Route terrain

Rugged and uneven upland paths

P Parking

National Park car park 2½ miles north of Dolgellau on road to Llanfachreth

OS maps

Landranger 124 (Porthmadog & Dolgellau), Explorer OL18 (Harlech, Porthmadog & Bala/y Bala)

GPS waypoints

⬛ SH 745 211
Ⓐ SH 744 212
Ⓑ SH 740 212
Ⓒ SH 735 204

This is one of the classic short walks of Snowdonia and is entirely on courtesy paths owned by the Nannau Estate, which permits public access. It is most important that the Countryside Code is observed and in particular that walkers keep to the waymarked paths and close all gates. The route is easy to follow, with plenty of waymarks and a series of information boards, and the gradients are modest. The views on this walk are magnificent, constantly changing as the route follows a circuit around the slopes of Foel Cynwch and Foel Faner, and every bend reveals new vistas over the Arans, Coed y Brenin Forest, the Mawddach Valley and estuary and Cadair Idris. The precipice itself is the western section of the walk, high above the Mawddach, along a path believed to have been made by sheep. The final section is a lovely walk along the shores of Llyn Cynwch. Walkers should note that the path surface is often uneven underfoot – watch your footing as well as the scenery.

Cadair Idris from Precipice Walk

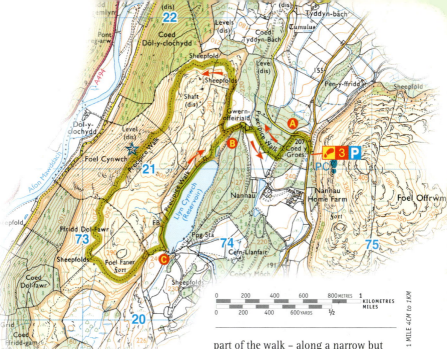

part of the walk – along a narrow but safe path through heather, bilberry, rocks and scree across the western edge of Foel Cynwch, which drops steeply to the Mawddach, giving magnificent distant views of the estuary and Cadair Idris.

Climb another ladder-stile, keep ahead, and as the path approaches the end of the ridge there are particularly fine views to be seen ahead over Dolgellau, the Mawddach Estuary and Cadair Idris. Turn half-left off the next ladder-stile onto a grassy path that curves gently to the left above a small rocky valley. Climb another ladder-stile and walk ahead with white waymark discs to reach a lakeside track beside Llyn Cynwch **C**.

Turn left along this, a delightful tree-lined path beside the peaceful reservoir, Dolgellau's water supply. Look back for excellent views of the distant Cadair Idris range. Continue straight ahead beyond the end of the lake, soon rejoining the initial outward leg of the walk at the ladder-stile at **B**. Simply retrace the paths from here to return to the car park. ●

From the car park turn left along the lane signposted to Hermon, and at a Precipice Walk sign **A** turn left along a track that heads gently up through conifers. The track turns right and later left in front of a stone cottage from where there is a view to the left of Nannau House, built in 1693 on the site of earlier houses and until the 1960s belonging to the Vaughan family, owners of the estate. It is now a hotel. Climb a ladder-stile, turn right and then turn left to head up to another ladder-stile **B**.

Climb it and walk ahead, drifting gradually right to walk beside a wall. Go sharp right around the waymarked corner, climb the ladder-stile and go ahead along the wall-side path beyond. To the right are grand views over rolling hills to the Arans, with Llanfachreth village and church as prominent landmarks. As the path curves to the left around the hill more superb views open up across the densely wooded slopes of Coed y Brenin Forest. After the next ladder-stile comes the precipice

SCALE 1:25 000 or 2½ INCHES to 1 MILE 4CM to 1KM

Ceunant Cynfal

Start

Bont Newydd, Ffestiniog: on A470 about 1¼ miles south-east of Llan Ffestiniog – turn down lane to south of bridge and bear right at a fork to a lay-by and footpath sign

Distance

3¾ miles (6km)

Height gain

755 feet (230m)

Approximate time

2 hours

Route terrain

Riverside paths, woodland, farmland

Parking

Small parking areas beside lane just to the west of Bont Newydd near a footpath sign.

OS maps

Landranger 124 (Porthmadog & Dolgellau), Explorer OL18 (Harlech, Porthmadog & Bala/y Bala)

GPS waypoints

SH 712 408
Ⓐ SH 705 411
Ⓑ SH 697 418
Ⓒ SH 687 415

This walk falls into three parts. The first and last stages go through woodlands that cloak both sides of the narrow ravine of Ceunant Cynfal; in contrast the middle section leads across fields and through more open country to the edge of Llan Ffestiniog. This middle part of the route is characterised by the superb views down the thickly wooded Vale of Ffestiniog and across to the 2,527ft (770m) bulk of Moelwyn Mawr.

Enter the woods at the footpath fingerpost at the lay-by, climb steps and go ahead up a steep slope a few paces, then turn right on an initially braided path through the woods. *Roots and stones make this rough underfoot so take particular care;* it clings to steep slopes high above the twisting gorge of Ceunant Cynfal, cleaved by a series of spectacular shoots and falls. Pass beneath a railway viaduct and follow the path, later between wall and fence, through these magnificent oak woods.

At a finger-post beside a fence and wooden gate, turn right to drop to and cross a footbridge Ⓐ, climb the steps at the far side, and follow the path through to a woodland edge kissing-gate and information panel.

A short diversion down the steps, left, leads to a viewing platform over Rhaeadr Cynfal, secreted in a particularly tortuous section of gorge. Return to and use the kissing-gate, walking ahead along a grassy path, by a wall on the right and above a sloping meadow, high up on the right-hand side of the valley. Go through a wooden gate and continue gently uphill by a wire fence on the right. Ahead is Moelwyn Mawr with the wall of the Llyn Stwlan Dam clearly visible. Go through a metal gate and walk ahead 20 paces to take a hand-gate on your left. Keep the wall on your right, go through a kissing-gate, drop to a plank bridge and a further kissing-gate from which rise half-left to another kissing-gate above a ruinous barn. Go through and turn right alongside a fence. Cross straight over the field road to use a gate into the main road beside a barn. Turn left, downhill.

At a sharp bend Ⓑ, take the track that forks left. Go through a wooden gate or climb a stile into a field road and remain on this. Go through a wooden gate and keep beside the wall on your right. Use the next corner-gate to put an old wall on your left; then use a third gate and bear left with a field road that shortly sweeps right, downhill beside a wall on your left. Near the slope foot, turn left through a broken wall, putting a wall on your right. Look ahead for a ladder-stile into a woodland path. This threads down to a stone step stile onto the main road. Turn left and cross Tal-y-bont Bridge **C**.

Take the finger-posted track on the left immediately past the bridge. This is a wide old track high above the river and is boggy for a while. It passes through gloomy conifer woods before a hand-gate brings the relief of airy oak woods. The path rises and falls. Go through a hand-gate and continue uphill, the path gradually emerging into steep bracken-covered pasture. Through two close-spaced gates and over a flat bridge, continue on the wide, level path across the flank of a steep, bracken-covered hillside with splendid views

Ceunant Cynfal

down into Ceunant Cynfal.

Keep left just before a field gate, shortly using a gate back into woodland. Cross a slab bridge and use a hand-gate, turning left beyond to follow the path along the woodland fringe, dropping to another gate and the four-way finger-post at **A**. From here turn right and retrace your steps back to the lay-by. ●

SCALE 1:25 000 or 2½ INCHES to 1 MILE *4CM to 1KM*

0	200	400	600	800 METRES	1
					KILOMETRES
					MILES
0	200	400	600 YARDS	½	

walk 5

Start
Tal-y-llyn

Distance
4 miles (6.3km)

Height gain
625 feet (190m)

Approximate time
2 hours

Route terrain
Farmland; hill slopes; road walking

Parking
Several lay-bys at the west end of the lake near Ty'n-y-cornel Hotel

OS maps
Landranger 124 (Porthmadog & Dolgellau), Explorer OL23 (Cadair Idris & Llyn Tegid)

GPS waypoints
SH 714 095
Ⓐ SH 710 096
Ⓑ SH 705 093
Ⓒ SH 709 100
Ⓓ SH 721 105
Ⓔ SH 728 104

Tal-y-llyn Lake (Llyn Mwyngil)

Tal-y-llyn Lake (Llyn Mwyngil in Welsh), hemmed in by sweeping mountainsides and sheltering below the southern slopes of Cadair Idris, is an outstandingly beautiful lake, as this circuit demonstrates. There are glorious and constantly changing views across it throughout the walk, but perhaps the finest are from the north side, where the path climbs up through woodland and then contours above the lake before descending to its low-lying eastern shores. The only climb – a steady and relatively short one – comes near the beginning.

Start near the **Ty'n-y-cornel Hotel** and walk along the road, with the lake on your right, towards the **Pen-y-bont Hote**l. Opposite the latter is the small, simple but appealing late 15th-century church of St Mary, noted for its fine timber roof. Turn right along a tarmac drive in front of the hotel and just before the drive curves right, turn left through a gate, at a public bridleway sign Ⓐ.

Head uphill along the left inside edge of sloping woodland, and at a fork take the right-hand uphill track to a T-junction Ⓑ. Turn sharp right and walk up the steepening path; at the next fork keep right, rising steadily through the woods. Cross diagonally over an old forestry road and trace the narrower path to the edge of the woods. Bear right through a gate beside a cattle-grid, continue more gently uphill along a broad track and where the track bends left to a farm, keep ahead to ford a stream and climb a ladder-stile.

Keep ahead to a footpath post, bear left to a ladder-stile and, despite the multitude of waymarks, do not climb it but turn right Ⓒ along a gently descending track, by a fence and hedge on the left. From this section are probably the finest of many fine views across Tal-y-llyn Lake to the encircling mountains. Go through the farther of two metal field gates, and then walk beside the fence at the top of the woods. As the trees fail, keep ahead on the track to the far side of the steep pasture and here turn downhill. Walk the woodland edge to find an in-field waymark pointing the way left to and through a gate into the trees.

Cross the footbridge and turn right through a wooden gate, then follow the fenced path, then rough track, behind the farmhouse and down to a tarred lane near the barns. Turn left,

Tal-y-llyn Lake

go through a metal gate and walk along this pleasantly tree-lined track as far as a public footpath sign where you bear right on to a sunken path **D**. Bear right again to cross a footbridge over a stream, and then head half-left, diagonally across the reedy meadows at the head of the lake – these will be very soggy in wet weather – to a small metal hand-gate. Use this, cross the footbridge and head half-left again, using yellow-topped posts to aid navigation to a stile. Cross this and the footbridge, and then look slightly left to spot a gate in the far banked hedge. Go through

this and walk beside a double fence on your right. At a footbridge, turn right, climb a stile and head across the small pasture to another stile leading directly onto the road **E**.

Turn right and follow the lakeside road back to the lay-by some 1¼ miles away. ●

SCALE 1:25000 or 2½ INCHES to 1 MILE 4CM to 1KM

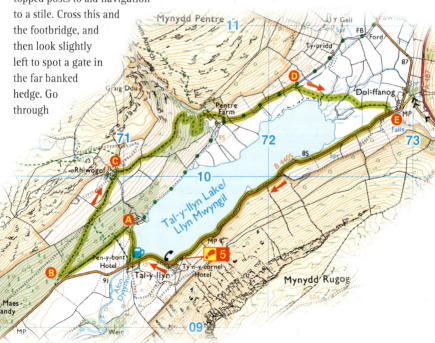

Capel Curig

Start
Capel Curig

Distance
4 miles (6.4km)

Height gain
655 feet (200m)

Approximate time
2½ hours

Route terrain
Rough pasture;
woodland; riverside
paths

Parking
National Park car park

OS maps
Landranger 115
(Snowdon/Yr Wyddfa),
Explorer OL17
(Snowdon/Yr Wyddfa)

GPS waypoints
SH 720 582
A SH 731 581
B SH 732 575
C SH 734 571
D SH 731 575
E SH 715 578
F SH 719 584

This relatively short and undemanding route around Capel Curig has fine views of the surrounding mountains and valleys, areas of woodland, and attractive riverside and lakeside walking. The highlight of the walk, given clear conditions, is the view of Snowdon across Llynnau Mymbyr, one of the classic views of North Wales.

Capel Curig Capel Curig is strung out along the A5 in the very heart of the grandest mountain terrain in Snowdonia, and with plenty of hotels, guest houses, pubs and cafés it is ideal for walkers, climbers and cyclists. Just to the west of the village is Plas y Brenin, the National Centre for Mountain Activities.

Walk down to the road junction and left again to cross the A5 to a stile/gate to the left of the war memorial and half-hidden 19th-century, neo-Norman St Curig's church. A well-constructed rocky path leads uphill across a field to a wall-gap. Cross the slab bridge beyond and bear right at the fork, soon joining a stone causeway across marshy pasture to a ladder-stile giving into woodland. Walk the woodland path, keeping right at a fork. The path undulates out of the trees and across a bracken-covered slope below Clogwynmawr, revealing views, right, across the Llugwy valley to shapely Moel Siabod. Climb the left-hand one of three ladder-stiles at a fenced corner and rise alongside a fence (right) across slabby pasture for about 500yds to reach a small concrete footbridge across a culverted stream **A**.

Do not cross this; instead turn sharp-right and walk alongside the stream, left, then a fence, to cross a slab-bridge. Pick up the line of a property wall/fence on your left, descending to climb a ladder-stile. Bend left to take a gate into a rough lane at a bend. Walk to your left for about 30 strides, and then fork left off the track onto a grassy path rising beside a fence, curving round to another ladder-stile. Climb it, later cross a track and descend to climb another ladder-stile into woodland. Continue downhill through this most attractive wood and take the right-hand path at a fork, descending quite steeply, following it around right- and left-hand bends to reach a ladder-stile to the left of a school **B**.

Climb the stile, turn left along the A5, passing the Tyn y Coed Hotel, and take the first turning on the right. Cross the bridge

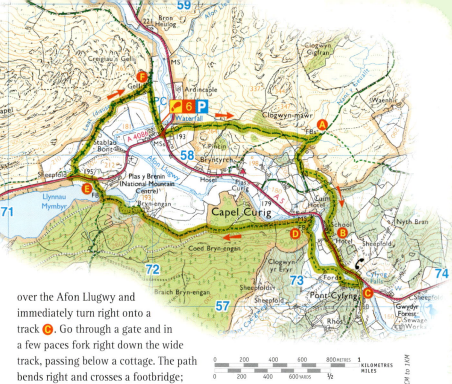

over the Afon Llugwy and immediately turn right onto a track **C**. Go through a gate and in a few paces fork right down the wide track, passing below a cottage. The path bends right and crosses a footbridge; from here head half-left to pass to the right of the old stone barn. Now remain on a riverside path heading upstream. Climb a ladder-stile into woodland and walk ahead to take the right-hand one of two gaps through a line of rocks. Beyond, rise gently with the path to a junction in front of the snout of a rock face. Fork right and wind with this riverside path through to a constriction above a sharp left-bend in the river **D**.

Immediately around the corner here is Cobden's Footbridge across the Afon Llugwy. Do not cross this but, rather, turn sharp left up a path to reach a fingerpost at a fork. Bear right here, the braided path rising gradually through the woods. Favour your right hand to pick up a singular path beside fencing above a steep drop and old lead mine; the river is far below. Descend steps and remain on the wide forestry track as it meanders through the superb Coed Bryn-engan woods.

At a major junction bear left for about 70 paces and then fork right

downhill, the compacted forestry road soon levels and you remain on this to and through a gate above two remote houses, shortly after passing the second of these you arrive at a path junction above the footbridge near to Plas y Brenin National Mountain Centre. Cross this and walk beside the boundary wall. To your left is one of the classic low-level views in Snowdonia, across Llynnau Mymbyr to the majestic Snowdon Horseshoe. Climb a ladder-stile onto the main road and turn left **E**.

As the road bends left, cross to the right and climb a ladder-stile, keep ahead along the rough field road and, at a fork, keep ahead-left, continuing along this track as it gradually bends right and passes through two metal gates. Pass beside the cottage and walk to the nearby ruined barn **F**. Turn sharp right here on another track, climb a ladder-stile and walk the tarred lane back to the start. ●

walk 7

Start

Penmaenpool

Distance

5 miles (8km)

Height gain

790 feet (240m)

Approximate time

2½ hours

Route terrain

Woodland; rough upland pastures; old railway trackbed through coastal marshland

Parking

National Park car park off A493

OS maps

Landranger 124 (Porthmadog & Dolgellau), Explorer OL18 (Harlech, Porthmadog & Bala/y Bala)

GPS waypoints

🖉 SH 695 185
Ⓐ SH 700 177
Ⓑ SH 681 169
Ⓒ SH 678 171
Ⓓ SH 670 176

Penmaenpool and the Mawddach Trail

This is an undemanding walk that for remarkably little effort provides outstanding views, especially of Cadair Idris and the Mawddach Estuary. It includes some fine woodland sections and finishes with a relaxing stroll along the south side of the estuary – acclaimed as one of the most beautiful in Europe – using the track of a disued railway.

Penmaenpool

*Who long for rest, who look for pleasure
Away from counter, court or school
O where live well your lease of leisure
But here, here at Penmaenpool.*

So wrote Gerard Manley Hopkins in 1876, but nowadays Penmaenpool is even quieter. Indeed it is hard to believe that this tiny hamlet at the southern end of a wooden toll bridge across the Mawddach was once an important shipping and shipbuilding centre. Both the railway that ran along the estuary from Barmouth Junction (now renamed Morfa Mawddach) to Dolgellau and the station at Penmaenpool had life spans of exactly a century, opened in 1865 and closed in 1965. At least this disused railway now serves useful purposes: the line as a footpath and the former signal-box at Penmaenpool as an RSPB Nature and Wildlife Centre.

🖉 From the car park entrance walk up to the main A493 and turn right towards Tywyn. In 100yds, look left for a flight of steps, cross carefully to these and ascend them, joining a woodland path. Remain on this to reach a driveway and gate. Slip to the right through this; then turn sharp left up the lane.

After about a quarter of a mile of steady climbing you'll reach a small pool on your left. On the right here is a waymarked path that rises steeply up through sporadic woodland. Trace this through to a stile near the edge of the woods. Beyond this, go ahead and then half-right along the old field road to approach a remote cottage Ⓐ.

Just before the gate, ignore a waymark that directs you through the gate to the cottage and instead take a concessionary waymarked path to the right along a field road. Trace this to and past the stone barn, beyond which a ladder-stile beside an open gateway beckons. Ahead are mouthwatering views of the great wall that is Cadair Idris. Use this stile/gateway and follow the field road, bending right to find a further ladder-stile and then continue to the distant farm complex and a T-junction in the farmyard.

Turn right to pass between the barns to a waymarked gateway. Turn half-left from this up along the line of an old hedgerow to find a marker post beneath a thorn tree. Here turn right along the field road, cross the stream at a ladder-stile and bend left to and through a collapsed wall. Head now to the gate and ladder-stile in the top left corner and continue ahead beside the fence; as this ends, head gradually right to join a grassy path rising across the hillside (there's a wooden pole on the near horizon as a marker). Cresting the ridge reveals inspiring views across the Mawddach Estuary to Cardigan Bay whilst behind are final glimpses of Cadair Idris.

Look ahead for a stone step-stile over the wall (waymark post here), climb it and go ahead for a very short distance before turning right along a rough, winding old field road. Remain on this all the way down, en route using three gates (two with ladder-stiles) to gain a

narrow tarred lane beside an old school **B**. Turn right and drop with this woodland lane to the main road **C**.

The way now is along the lane virtually opposite, signed for Abergwynant Farm. Follow this alongside the tumbling waters of the Afon Gwynant (left) to reach an arched bridge. Remain on the right bank of the river, taking the tarred track to a pair of gates at a bend. Go through the left-hand one and straight on to a waymarked gate into the woodland edge. Turn left on the forestry road above the river, remaining on this for about 500 yds to a major fork. Here keep ahead-left, walking through to a gateway giving access to the old trackbed **D**.

Turn right on the route of the old line and walk upstream for just over 1½ miles to Penmaenpool – with grand views across the Mawddach Estuary all the while. Just before the end you pass through a wooded gully, crossing the neck of the headland of Penmaenpool; continue through a kissing-gate to the car park. ●

SCALE 1:27777 or 2¼ INCHES to 1 MILE 3.6CM to 1KM

0	200	400	600	800 METRES	1
					KILOMETRES
0	200	400	600 YARDS	½	MILES

Start

Rhyd Ddu

Distance

5 miles (8km)

Height gain

870 feet (265m)

Approximate time

2½ hours

Route terrain

Rough pasture; forest; a little road walking

Parking

At start (Pay and Display)

OS maps

Landranger 115 (Snowdon/Yr Wyddfa), Explorer OL17 (Snowdon/Yr Wyddfa)

GPS waypoints

SH 571 525
Ⓐ SH 566 526
Ⓑ SH 557 513
Ⓒ SH 575 508
Ⓓ SH 576 514
Ⓔ SH 582 524

Llyn y Gader and Beddgelert Forest

This walk is through scenery that lies just to the west of Snowdon, and the last part of it uses a section of the Rhyd Ddu Path, which is one of the most popular routes to the summit of Wales' highest mountain. For much of the way the austere Llyn y Gader is in sight, and there are dramatic views of Mynydd Mawr, the Nantlle ridge and Moel Hebog (Walk 16) to the west, and Yr Aran, the most southerly peak of the Snowdon range, to the east. The route also touches the northern fringes of the extensive Beddgelert Forest.

From the car park cross the road and go through a metal kissing-gate at a public footpath sign opposite. As you walk along a slate path there is a striking view ahead of the precipitous cliffs of Y Garn, the easterly end of the Nantlle ridge. On reaching the Afon Gwyrfai, follow the path to the left and then turn right to cross a footbridge over the river.

Climb a ladder-stile beyond which you reach the access track to a white-washed cottage (Tal y Llyn). Cross the track, and take to a narrow path through rushes and across rough pasture until you rejoin the access. Turn right and follow it out to the B4418 Ⓐ. Immediately turn left through a metal gate, at a public bridleway sign, and continue along a path by a low wall and wire fence on the right.

Go through a hand-gate and rise to a gate, ladder-stile and another gate. Go through and climb up to a boulder with a white arrow painted on it. Just past this keep half-left on a gently rising path (not the one steeply ahead), further painted arrows on boulders confirming the way, although they are not as distinct as they were of old.

On this part of the route are fine views right, to the Nantlle Ridge and ahead to Moel Hebog, whilst to the left, shapely Yr Aran rises beyond Llyn y Gader. Step over a stream, walk to and through a gate, step over another stream and bear half-right to climb more steeply and pass the foot of a spectacular water chute. The path levels out to reach a ladder-stile and gate into Beddgelert Forest. Go through and keep ahead on the path, pass through a wall gap and descend to a wide forestry road Ⓑ.

Turn left along this, initially through woods and then alongside a fence (left) beside reedy pastures. Keep right at the bend where a path leaves to your left. At the next fork keep left

The imposing profile of Y Garn

to reach a T-junction. Turn left and walk this forestry road past a barrier to reach the main road **C**, crossing the track of the Welsh Highland Railway on the way.

Turn left and after nearly 800yds, turn right through a metal gate at a public footpath sign **D** to Snowdon. Walk along a tarmac drive which bends left up to Ffridd Uchaf Farm. Pass through a metal gate, turn right between farm buildings and bear left to a hand-gate beside a yard gate. Use the hand-gate and walk up beside the conifer plantation on your left, go through a metal gate and continue uphill.

To the right are grand views of Snowdon, and to the left Llyn y Gader, Y Garn and the Nantlle Ridge come into view again. Climb a ladder-stile, keep ahead across grassy moorland – although the path is indistinct in places, there are regular marker-stones – and pass to the right of an outcrop of rocks to reach a T-junction in front of a metal gate **E**. Turn left along the old quarry road here, shortly passing by (but not using) a kissing-gate on your right

signed 'Footpath to Snowdon'. You're now following the Rhyd Ddu Path; descend between rocks to a ladder-stile. Climb it and as you continue steadily downhill along a winding path, glorious views open up looking along the length of Llyn Cwellyn towards Caernarfon and the Menai Strait.

Climb more stiles, keep ahead between old quarry workings, and continue to a gate at the railway line. Cross the line with care, and turn left along a track back to the car park at the start.

SCALE 1:25000 or 2½ INCHES to 1 MILE 4CM to 1KM

0	200	400	600	800 METRES	1
					KILOMETRES
					MILES
0	200	400	600 YARDS	½	

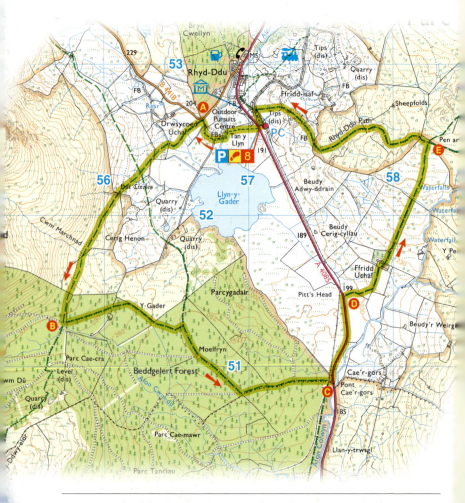

Pared y Cefn-hir and
Cregennen lake

Slightly harder walks of 3 – 4 hours

Lledr valley

Start
Dolwyddelan

Distance
6 miles (9.4km)

Height gain
1,115 feet (340m)

Approximate time
3 hours

Route terrain
Woodland trails; riverside paths; farmland; some road walking

Parking
Car park at edge of village

OS maps
Landranger 115 (Snowdon/Yr Wyddfa), Explorer OL18 (Harlech, Porthmadog & Bala/y Bala)

GPS waypoints
SH 737 521
Ⓐ SH 739 520
Ⓑ SH 772 537
Ⓒ SH 770 538
Ⓓ SH 756 537

This is a walk that provides a succession of outstanding views of the surrounding mountains, especially of Moel Siabod, which lies across the valley and of the more distant Snowdon massif, plus attractive woodland and riverside walking, for only a modest effort. The first half is along a broad, undulating trail, much of it through woodland, and the return is by tree-lined paths and lanes, and across lush meadows bordering the lovely River Lledr.

Leave the car park and at the road turn left again to cross the railway bridge, then bear left into High Street. Follow this lane uphill and on reaching a row of cottages on the right, turn left onto a gravel track Ⓐ.

Keep along this clear, broad, winding and gently undulating track for the next 2½ miles. At the start there are abandoned slate quarries, and for much of the way the track passes through attractive woodland. The more open stretches provide superb views to the left across the Lledr valley, with Snowdon and Moel Siabod prominent on the skyline, plus the impressively sited Dolwyddelan Castle.

The place at which you finally leave this forestry road Ⓑ is not waymarked, and easy to miss. Shortly after coming close to and above the railway, pass above a series of small, walled fields and collapsed buildings visible close-by down to your left. About 150yds past the end of the last one, a very narrow path angles sharply back to your left (to confirm that you're in the right place, there's also one forking off acutely to the right, a few strides farther on).

Turn sharp left here; the path parallels the forestry trail for a short distance, then widens into a woodland path and falls to pass beneath a railway bridge. Bear left and remain on the path, dropping to a ladder-stile to the right of the Tan-Aeldroch farm  **C**. Cross the stile and go ahead a few paces before bearing left at a fingerpost 'River Walk to Dolwyddelan' beside the gateway to the farm. A few strides farther on, pass through a gate giving onto a narrow, seasonally overgrown path that drops down to become a stony, slabbed riverside way.

Remain on this to enter woodland; in a farther 100yds fork right at a waymark post, taking the lower path which is uneven underfoot, so exercise care as you walk through this lovely, gorged section of the Lledr valley.

Occasional waymarked posts confirm you're on the right path; eventually you'll reach a waymarked wooden hand-gate through a wall. Use this, and a metal gate a short distance away, beyond which the path hugs a ledge between the river and the railway embankment before traversing woodland pasture.

An outdoor centre (Lledr Hall) appears in trees off to your right. At the reedy field-end, go through an old metal gate and cross a driveway **D**, to gain a rising path that climbs to join a tarred drive to the left of a hotel. Bear left and at the nearby bend fork left

SCALE 1:25 000 or 2½ INCHES to 1 MILE 4CM to 1KM

0   200   400   600   800 METRES   **1**
KILOMETRES
MILES
0   200   400   600 YARDS   ½

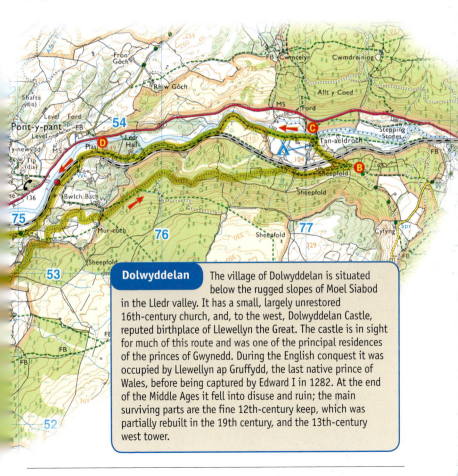

Dolwyddelan The village of Dolwyddelan is situated below the rugged slopes of Moel Siabod in the Lledr valley. It has a small, largely unrestored 16th-century church, and, to the west, Dolwyddelan Castle, reputed birthplace of Llewellyn the Great. The castle is in sight for much of this route and was one of the principal residences of the princes of Gwynedd. During the English conquest it was occupied by Llewellyn ap Gruffydd, the last native prince of Wales, before being captured by Edward I in 1282. At the end of the Middle Ages it fell into disuse and ruin; the main surviving parts are the fine 12th-century keep, which was partially rebuilt in the 19th century, and the 13th-century west tower.

along a surfaced lane, which leads to and past Pont-y-pant Station to where it ends at a farm. Keep ahead through a metal gate and walk along an undulating track, later keeping beside the railway line on the right. Pass through a gate, turn right to pass under the railway line once more, and then turn left along a path across lovely riverside meadows. Now come more splendid views of the river, Moel Siabod and Snowdon.

Pass to the right of farm buildings, and keep ahead along a track, passing by an attractive old clapper-bridge over the Lledr on the right. The tarmac track continues across meadows, keeps to the left of another farm – there are gates to negotiate here – and leads directly back to the starting point. ●

The Lledr Valley

Gwydyr Forest and Trefriw

walk 10

🖊 **Start**	
Llanrwst	
🚩 **Distance**	
6¼ miles (9.9km)	
⛰ **Height gain**	
870 feet (265m)	
🕐 **Approximate time**	
3 hours	
👟 **Route terrain**	
Meadows; woodland; some road walking	
🅿 **Parking**	
In Llanrwst	
🧭 **OS maps**	
Landranger 115 (Snowdon/Yr Wyddfa), Explorer OL17 (Snowdon/Yr Wyddfa)	
🗓 **GPS waypoints**	
🏁 SH 798 616	
Ⓐ SH 798 614	
Ⓑ SH 796 607	
Ⓒ SH 789 609	
Ⓓ SH 781 616	
Ⓔ SH 776 616	
Ⓕ SH 780 631	
Ⓖ SH 792 622	

The first and last parts of the walk are across attractive meadows bordering the River Conwy; most of the remainder is through woodland on the eastern slopes of Gwydyr Forest, from where there is a succession of fine views over the Conwy valley. Historic interest is provided by three churches, a 15th-century courthouse and a 17th-century bridge. Some climbing is involved through the forest, but none of it is too steep or strenuous.

> **Llanrwst** The pleasant market town of Llanrwst lies on the eastern bank of the River Conwy, here spanned by a fine three-arched bridge, built in 1636 and possibly designed by Inigo Jones. On the west side of the bridge is Tu-hwnt-i'r-bont, a 15th-century former courthouse, now owned by the National Trust and used as a gift shop and tearoom. The imposing church, largely rebuilt in the 1880s, is noted for its carved rood screen and loft, and for the adjacent Gwydir Chapel, built in the 17th century as the mausoleum for the Gwynne family of Gwydir Castle. At one time the large stone coffin in it was thought to be that of Llewellyn the Great.

🖊 The walk starts in the market place in the town centre. Walk along the main road in the Betws-y-coed direction, turn right to cross the old bridge over the River Conwy and immediately turn left at a public footpath sign Ⓐ, along a tarmac path. Continue beside the river – a delightful stretch of riverside walking with grand views upstream – going through a metal kissing-gate and keeping ahead to a stile.

After climbing the stile, turn right along the edge of a field up to a ladder-stile. Climb this and turn right along a road. At a sign to Gwydyr Uchaf Chapel Ⓑ, turn sharp left up a tarmac drive and where the drive bends equally sharply to the right, keep ahead – just to the right of a bench – along a steep uphill path through trees, here entering Gwydyr Forest. The path curves left then right to reach a broad track; turn sharp right along it and at a fork immediately ahead, take the right-hand lower track. From this track there are attractive views through the trees to the right, over Llanrwst and the Conwy valley. The track passes above Gwydyr Uchaf chapel to which a short detour can be made by turning right along a track and, where it bends right, keeping ahead down a shady path, climbing two stiles. Originally built for the Gwynne family in 1604, it has a fine painted ceiling. The home of the Gwynnes, the much-restored Tudor mansion of Gwydir Castle, is nearby.

Return to the main route, where the track continues along the edge of the forest to emerge on to a lane at a junction **C**. Take the narrow lane ahead, signposted to Llanrhychwyn, cross a stream, and a ladder-stile on the right gives access to the Grey Mare's Tail waterfall, after decent rains a spectacular, graceful twin falls.

The lane soon starts to climb quite steeply; in ¾ mile you'll reach the edge of the woods **D**. On the left here, and immediately within the woods, walk along a rising, waymarked path and climb a nearby ladder-stile. Go ahead beside a fallen wall and then a wire fence, soon emerging into a small pasture. Keep along the left edge to use a stile beside a wooden gate – the way is then a wide grassy track through open oakwoods. Take another stile beside a gateway into pasture and walk ahead towards the far left corner. Just up from this is a stile into a wide, fenced track through a strand of trees.

Keep left to use a metal gate and then walk the field road to gain a rough lane just right of the farm **E**. The way is right, along the lane.

It is, however, a rewarding detour to find the remote and ancient church at Llanrhychwyn. To do so, turn left and take the track to the right of the farmhouse. Look immediately on your right for a waymarked kissing-gate onto a path up steps. Take this and climb to a second kissing-gate. Pass through a third kissing-gate near a cottage and rise to a fourth, just to the right of the little church visible in trees on the hillside. Dedicated to St Rhychwyn, it too has connections to Llywelyn Fawr

(the Great) and is a superb example of a totally unspoilt simple, early-medieval rural church, complete with slate-slabbed floor and lit by candles.

Return to the lane by the farm and walk it through to the crossroads in the tiny hamlet. Keep ahead along a narrow lane, in the Trefriw direction, and there are impressive views of the houses of Trefriw ahead, clinging to the sides of the steep hillside above the valley, as the lane descends steeply into the village. Pass by the first few houses; at the second public footpath sign on your right (just before a white-painted house, Y Wern, on the left) turn down a short, tarred ramp onto an enclosed path, dropping to a lane. Bear left down this to a junction; here go ahead along a path beside a garage and cross a footbridge over the Afon Crafnant. Walk along the winding path to a road and here turn right to a junction above an old chapel. Turn right to reach the main road in Trefriw **F**, turn right here to reach the village centre.

> **Trefriw** Trefriw is noted for its woollen mill where visitors can watch the various stages in the production of tweeds and tapestries. Just to the north of the village is the Victorian spa of Trefriw Wells.

Turn left opposite Trefriw Woollen Mills, passing a parking area. Continue along a straight, tarmac drive for just under 1 mile to reach a suspension bridge over the River Conwy. Do not cross it but turn right over a stile **G** and walk along the top of an embankment. Pass by one stile to reach a second above gates. Climb this and turn left to climb a stile, and cross a flat bridge; beyond this follow a path along the left edge of a series of fields and over a succession of stiles. Eventually, climb a ladder-stile and turn left along an enclosed, hedge-lined track which bears right and continues to a road. Turn left and re-cross the old bridge over the river to return to the centre of Llanrwst. ●

The River Conwy at Llanrwst

SCALE 1:25000 or 2½ INCHES to 1 MILE 4CM to 1KM

walk 11

Coed-y-brenin

Start
Ganllwyd

Distance
5¼ miles (8.3km)

Height gain
755 feet (230m)

Approximate time
3 hours

Route terrain
Woodland trails; some road walking

Parking
National Trust car park with toilets at southern end of village

OS maps
Landranger 124 (Porthmadog & Dolgellau), Explorer OL18 (Harlech, Porthmadog & Bala/y Bala)

GPS waypoints
- SH 726 243
- Ⓐ SH 727 248
- Ⓑ SH 736 275
- Ⓒ SH 734 275

Almost the whole route is through the woodlands of the vast Coed-y-brenin Forest, an easy walk mostly along broad, clear tracks with only relatively gentle climbing. From the higher and more open parts, there are fine views over the surrounding mountains of the Rhinog and Cadair Idris ranges. The walk visits two spectacular waterfalls: Rhaeadr Mawddach and Pistyll Cain, before taking a leisurely loop through the woodlands.

Leave the car park and turn right, passing the village school. Beyond the lay-by, fork right down the 'No Through Road' at the speed de-restriction signs. Cross the bridge over the Afon Eden Ⓐ and bear right, following this tarred lane past a telephone exchange and into magnificent fir woods. At a left bend in 800yds, fork right down a wide rough lane leading to the Pont Cae'n Coed car park and passing a Geology Trail board to reach and cross a long footbridge spanning the Mawddach. Turn left along the forestry road beyond.

In 400yds, fork left past a gate, the route still following the gorge of the Mawddach and confirmed by yellow-topped posts. In just over 800yds, again fork left at a junction; the roadway eventually bends sharply left, in due course emerging from the trees to unveil a view down into the gorge and the Rhaeadr Mawddach Falls Ⓑ.

Gwynfynydd Gold Mine

In the wooded hills above Rhaeadr Mawddach is the Gwynfynydd Gold Mine. Gold was first found here in 1863 but it was not until 1887 that it became fully exploited under William Pritchard Morgan, the Welsh gold king. The mine closed in 1916, reopened in the 1930s and worked again until 1999.

About 150yds past this point through a gate and opposite a bridleway finger-post, fork left down a steep track (waymarked council road, and marked by a white and yellow topped post) to reach and cross a stone bridge over the Afon Mawddach. Your way is left along the roadway at the far side, passing above the Rhaeadr Mawddach.

The route continues to the left, heading downhill and bearing right to keep beside the Afon Gain near its confluence with the Mawddach. On the left is the site of the gold-mine mill. It closed a year after the mine, in 1917, was rebuilt in the 1930s but burned down in 1935 before it was completed. Sweep left across the wide, rusty metal bridge over the Afon Gain; to your right is the spectacular Pistyll Cain **C**, after decent rain one of the most impressive falls in Snowdonia.

Remain on the rough road, eventually passing the buildings at Ferndale holiday cottages. Beyond a gateway the track becomes a tarred lane, shortly reaching the Tyddyn Gwladys forestry car park. All that now remains is to follow the tarred lane back to Ganllwyd. ●

SCALE 1:25000 or 2½ INCHES to 1 MILE 4CM to 1KM

The River Mawddach near Ganllwyd

Vale of Ffestiniog

walk 12

Start
Rhŷd-y-sarn

Distance
5¾ miles (9km)

Height gain
900 feet (275m)

Approximate time
3 hours

Route terrain
Woodland; riverside pastures; road walking

P **Parking**
Parking and picnic area, beside A496, 800yds north of its junction with B4391 – look for the telephone box by a lay-by near cottages

OS maps
Landranger 124 (Porthmadog & Dolgellau), Explorer OL18 (Harlech, Porthmadog & Bala/y Bala)

GPS waypoints
SH 690 422
Ⓐ SH 680 423
Ⓑ SH 665 411
Ⓒ SH 664 408
Ⓓ SH 667 412
Ⓔ SH 687 416
Ⓕ SH 692 419

The first part of the walk is through the delightful, dense, steep-sided woodlands that cloak the northern slopes of the Vale of Ffestiniog, part of the Coedydd Maentwrog National Nature Reserve. There is a succession of superb views down the vale and on several occasions the path crosses the track of the steam-hauled Ffestiniog Railway. After descending into the valley and making a brief detour into Maentwrog, the route continues by the Afon Dwyryd before a final wooded stretch. Although this is not a lengthy or strenuous walk, there is quite a lot of climbing, especially in the first stage.

Facing the picnic site – on the opposite side of the road from the parking area – turn right, almost immediately turn left along a track, at a public footpath sign, and go through a metal gate. The track curves to the left; where it ends, keep ahead along a path to go through a gate. Keep ahead on the woodland path, bending left to a gate leading into the Coed Cymerau National Nature Reserve. This is an area of oak woodland, probably a remnant of the vast woodlands that used to cover much of North Wales.

Head uphill beside the lovely surging river – there are lots of small waterfalls – turn left over a footbridge and continue climbing quite steeply. The woodland becomes a conifer plantation. Walking by a second Nature Reserve board, stay on the main path, stepping over a brook and shortly passing through a broken wall. At the top of the woods climb the ladder-stile and walk ahead beside a wall and through high bracken. Climb a further ladder-stile and turn left; shortly bear right up a rough lane, and follow this along the woodland edge, keeping left at a fork Ⓐ.

The old lane levels out at a point where the trackbed of the old route of the Ffestiniog Railway is reached – there's a ruined overbridge a short way ahead. Turn sharp-left to walk along the trackbed, marked by old wooden sleepers. Go through a gate into Dduallt Station and walk ahead (crossing the nearest railway line) to pass to the right of the station building. Just beyond the abandoned house on the right, re-cross the line, climb the ladder-stile and turn left along a path parallel to the railway. Go under the railway bridge and follow the path through bracken and via two wall gaps to another ladder-stile. On this part of the walk the views down the wooded Vale of

Ffestiniog and over the surrounding mountains are superb and, at times, the buildings of Trawsfynydd Nuclear Power Station appear on the horizon.

Climb the stile, cross the line again, climb another ladder-stile and turn right on to a path that descends along the side of the valley to join a track in front of a house. Keep ahead along the steadily descending track – it later becomes a tarmac track – and where it makes a U-bend to the left, keep ahead over a stile at a public footpath sign. Head down to cross a stream below a waterfall, continue downhill to a kissing-gate, go through, bear left and descend steeply to a concrete track. Turn right uphill, passing to the left of a house, and cross a footbridge over a stream. Bear half-left off the bridge on a level path through to a hand-gate. Go through this and trace the undulating path through superb woodlands, gradually dropping to reach a tarred lane **B**.

Turn right to the main road and turn left along it. Just before the bridge across the Afon Dwyryd the route turns left, through a kissing-gate and onto an embankment **C**.

*For a brief detour into Maentwrog, and to visit **The Grapes** inn, keep ahead and fork right, cross the river and at a T-junction turn right through the village, built in the early 19th century by William Oakley, a local slate magnate. The spire of the Victorian church is appropriately covered in slate. Return to the bridge and go through the kissing-gate onto the embankment.*

Walk along the top of the embankment. Along this stretch of the route you can enjoy the fine views looking up the wooded vale, framed by mountains and with lush riverside meadows on either side. On approaching the river the path curves

left to a gate **D**. Go through, turn right and keep along a quiet, attractive lane for the next 1½ miles – initially beside the river, then bending right to cross it, and finally continuing by a tributary stream (Afon Cynfal) up to a road.

Turn sharp right to a junction, then turn sharp left, in the Ffestiniog direction, and at a public footpath sign, turn right over a stone stile **E**. Head uphill through woodland, climb a ladder-stile, keep ahead to emerge from the trees and walk alongside a wall. At the tumbled corner, step through the gap and turn left, wall now on your left, and walk through to a stile onto a road. Turn right and walk uphill for 200yds; turn left at a public footpath sign **F** and then go through a gate and walk down the enclosed path. After going

SCALE 1:25000 or 2½ INCHES to 1 MILE 4CM to 1KM

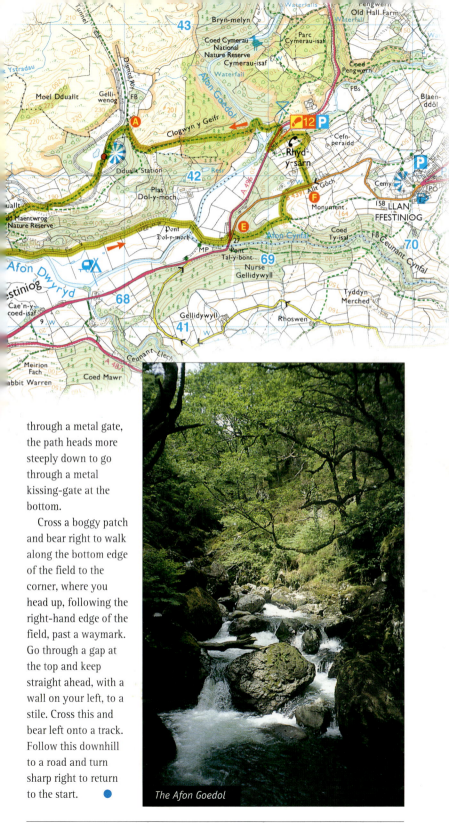

through a metal gate, the path heads more steeply down to go through a metal kissing-gate at the bottom.

Cross a boggy patch and bear right to walk along the bottom edge of the field to the corner, where you head up, following the right-hand edge of the field, past a waymark. Go through a gap at the top and keep straight ahead, with a wall on your left, to a stile. Cross this and bear left onto a track. Follow this downhill to a road and turn sharp right to return to the start. ●

The Afon Goedol

Cregennen Lakes (Llynnau Cregennen)

Start
Arthog

Distance
5½ miles (8.6km)

Height gain
1,100 feet (335m)

Approximate time
3½ hours

Route terrain
Woodland; farmland; some lane walking

P Parking
National Park car park at start

OS maps
Landranger 124 (Porthmadog & Dolgellau), Explorer OL23 (Cadair Idris & Llyn Tegid)

GPS waypoints
SH 640 148
Ⓐ SH 649 138
Ⓑ SH 663 136
Ⓒ SH 655 146
Ⓓ SH 645 140
Ⓔ SH 638 143

The Cregennen Lakes lie in a setting of outstanding beauty largely unsuspected by travellers along the estuary road below. This is a craggy, twisted, hummocky and charmingly satisfying place, reached in this figure-of-eight walk by the delights of the Arthog woodland and its many waterfalls. The views, in spite of nearby high mountains are excellent, and extend as far as the Lleyn Peninsula, beyond the golden sands of the Mawddach Estuary.

There is a small car park and picnic area down a gated track leading seaward from Arthog, beside the Mawddach Trail. From it, turn right, back towards the main road, but walk only as far as a ladder-stile on the left to gain access to a raised sea defence embankment, which will lead you out beside Arthog river, to the road. Turn left briefly, and walk to the entrance to St Catherine's church, there crossing the road to a signed footpath rising, initially by steps, into broad-leaved woodland. This is quite special, a Site of Special Scientific Interest (SSSI), and in springtime bright with bluebells.

As the path climbs steeply for a while, and then at a more relaxed gradient to reach a broad horizontal track. Turn left, and a few strides further on, at a waymark, branch right onto a rising path, which climbs beside the many Arthog waterfalls, cascading in a shaded dell. The water flows from Llyn Cyri, high in the embrace of Crag-y-llyn, to be encountered later.

Towards the top of the climb, the path swings right, away from the falls for a while before turning back, and then up to a ladder-stile spanning a high, mossy wall. The path is reluctant to leave the woodland, and skims along the top edge of the wooded gorge, but does finally leave it at a ladder-stile, close by an ancient clapper bridge Ⓐ spanning the stream.

The sudden, open view is breathtaking, and the mountain in the background is Tyrau Mawr, which with its neighbour Craig-y-llyn, soon to come into view, forms a massive wall running south-west from Cadair Idris. On the right, over the clapper bridge, lie the remains of Llys Bradwen (Bradwen's Court). Here stood the court of Ednywain ab Bradwen, leader of one of the Fifteen Tribes of Gwynedd who lived here early in the 12th century, in the time of Prince Gruffydd ab Cynan.

Pared y Cefn-hir and Cregennen lake

Continue beside the stream as far as a turning up to Pant-y-llan farm, and follow the track out to meet an unfenced lane, with Craig-y-llyn now in view on the right. Here, turn left and follow the lane as far as the first turning on the left, signed for Cregennen Lakes **B**: the corner can be shortcut on a brief grassy path. The lane brings first one and then a second lake into view set against the distinctly craggy profile of Pared y Cefn-hir (the Wall of the Long Ridge), to which strong walkers may be tempted to make a visit.

Keep on, past the lakes and a car park (toilets), still following the road, which shortly starts to descend. Go past a holiday cottage, then, as the lane swings sharply to the right **C**, leave it for a signed footpath that climbs beside a wall. At a wall junction go through two gaps on the left, and then cross a ladder-stile and bear right following a waymarked path across rough pasture.

This leads to another ladder-stile, beyond which the grassy path continues across more rough pasture and into a brief section of walled track.

Pared y Cefn-hir and Cregennen

This minor summit supports an Iron Age defended enclosure overlooking the nearby ancient Ffordd Ddu track, flanked by numerous standing stones, and in turn overtopped by mountain-top burial cairns on Tyrau Mawr and Craig-y-llyn. All of which tells of prehistoric times. To casual view, however, it is simply scenery that is first rate, and the temptation to linger by the lakes is not easily ignored.

The name 'Cregennen' derives from 'crog-gangen', which translates as 'hanging branch'. Criminals who were convicted of crimes at Llys Bradwen were executed on the branch of a nearby oak tree. Today, the lakes are owned by the National Trust, and are popular for trout fishing.

Throughout this stretch there are splendid views northwards over the Mawddach Estuary to Barmouth. To the right of Barmouth lie the rugged hills that form the southern end of the Rhinogs. In 1834, deep among these hills gold veins were discovered. Gold mining work began in 1847, and in 1854 a valuable gold seam was discovered at the Clogau copper mine.

The mining work has now come to an end, but a local company, Clogau, continues to sell jewellery made from Welsh gold.

At the end of the enclosed section, turn right parallel with the wall, which shortly feeds into another walled track at a gate. Stay with this until you can leave it at a waymark by branching down through bracken to the clapper

The Clapper Bridge with Tyrau Mawr beyond

bridge Ⓐ passed earlier in the walk. Turn right, and pass the top of the Arthog woodland, which offers a direct and speedy way back to the start, if necessary.

Keep past the woodland stile to a metal gate beyond which you intercept a surfaced lane. Turn right, descending, and continue following the lane until it descends steeply to the right. Here, leave it for a bridleway on the left Ⓓ for Tyn y Graig and Merddyn. The path follows an agreeable course, and then starts to descend through more

woodland, and finally runs down past Ty Coch to reach the valley road.

Walk to the right along the road for about 250yds, then leave the road for a bridleway on the left Ⓔ that leads down to the Mawddach Trail. Turn right along the trail and shortly complete the walk. ●

> ### Mawddach Trail
> The Mawddach Trail makes use of the trackbed of the Great Western Railway, operational from 1868 until 1965. The section of the line from Dolgellau to Morfa Mawddach is now owned by the National Park Authority.

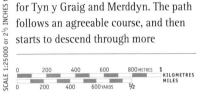

SCALE 1:25000 or 2½ INCHES to 1 MILE 4CM to 1KM

```
0    200   400   600   800 METRES    1
                                     KILOMETRES
                                     MILES
0    200   400   600 YARDS    ½
```

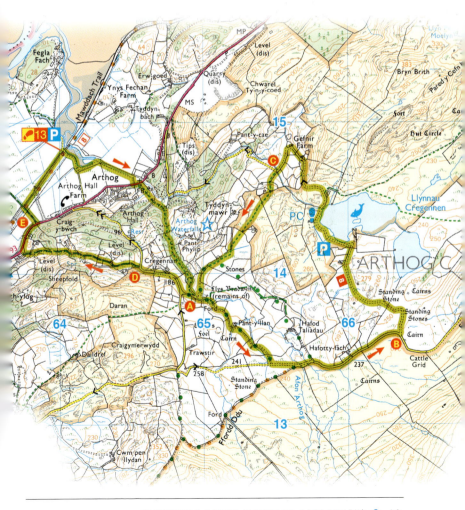

Start
Tanygrisiau

Distance
5½ miles (8.6km)

Height gain
1,380 feet (420m)

Approximate time
3½ hours

Route terrain
Rocky tracks through industrial remains; moorland

Parking
Car park on the outskirts of Tanygrisiau, immediately to the west of the bridge that spans the stream issuing from Llyn Cwmorthin

OS maps
Landrangers 115 (Snowdon/Yr Wyddfa) and 124 (Porthmadog & Dolgellau), Explorers OL17 (Snowdon/Yr Wyddfa) and OL18 (Harlech, Porthmadog & Bala/y Bala)

GPS waypoints
SH 683 452
Ⓐ SH 678 460
Ⓑ SH 665 462
Ⓒ SH 666 456
Ⓓ SH 667 452
Ⓔ SH 665 443

Tanygrisiau and Rhosydd

This walk is all about industrial heritage and archaeology, and it might be supposed, given the reputation the area around Blaenau Ffestiniog has for industrial dereliction, that the walk would lack essential qualities. Remarkably, in spite of the remnants of that history, the scenery remains inspiring, rugged throughout, and with stunning views of familiar mountains from unfamiliar angles. There is a latent melancholy about the scenes you encounter, a place where the silence is often penetrated only by the echoes of the past. It is, in short, quite special, concluding in the lee of those great twins Moelwyn Mawr and Moelwyn Bach.

From the car park turn left and cross the bridge, walk on a little and take the first turning on the left in front of Rhesdai Dolrhedyn Terrace, following a narrow lane up and left to a gate giving onto a broad slaty path climbing beside a waterfall in a ravine.

Now follow the track upwards, and, at the top of the first rise, as the track levels, branch left at a waymark, over a bridge into

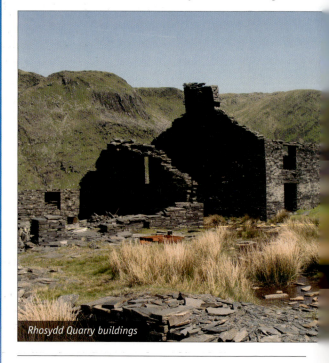

Rhosydd Quarry buildings

a small pine plantation, and follow a path, right, to a gate beyond which the on-going path ambles on pleasantly to a derelict building at the outflow of Llyn Cwmorthin Ⓐ. The same point can be reached by remaining on the original track, and crossing the outflow on a slab bridge. Apart from the industrial heritage, there is much geological interest here, too, with both sedimentary and volcanic rocks in profusion, all bearing the tell-tale marks of glaciation.

Ahead, the lily dappled waters of the lake are set against the rugged slopes of Allt Fawr and Moel Druman. The track leads on easily, passing the lake and more derelict buildings to venture farther into the cwm, until, finally, it reaches a gate at the foot of a steep, curving ramp. Take the ramp upwards, stony underfoot, and rising in two distinct stages through spoil heaps and ancient buildings of indeterminate purpose, until it pops out onto the surprisingly wide and open Rhosydd

Rhosydd Quarry

Slate was first discovered at Rhosydd in the 1830s, when quarrying commenced on a very small scale. This early enterprise was enlarged and deepened over the years to a depth of more than 200 feet, and as workings went deeper, adits and tunnels were driven in to win more slate and drain the workings. Over time, the quarry developed to encompass 14 floors underground, with a total of 170 chambers from which the slate was won.

The quarry was operated by a string of different owners, but the uncertainties of the slate trade, the problems of securing investment, geological problems and dangerous underground working practices also brought intermittent periods of closure and industrial unrest. Peak output occurred in the 1880s, when over 6,000 tons per year of saleable slate was mined by more than 200 workers.

The First World War brought a period of complete closure followed by re-opening in 1919 and a brief flurry of activity. A slow lingering existence followed until final closure in 1930. The life of the quarry had effectively ended and the scrap men moved in. The final humiliation was the demolition of quarry buildings to recover workable slate. This accounts for the stacks of slate you will still find, and the ruinous condition of much of the site.

plateau, opposite the remaining buildings Ⓑ. Note, ahead and beyond the buildings, another stony ramp rising along the flank of a tumbledown spoil heap. This is the onward route. But for now, take time to explore these buildings that once resounded to the clamour of man's industry.

Continue the walk by heading for that ramp behind the buildings, first passing a water-sodden adit, a huge man-made tunnel that it is not wise to venture inside. The rising ramp, leads up in instalments, and finally reaches the top site of this industrial landscape, below the swelling bulk of Moelwyn Mawr, with shapely Cnicht behind you to the right. Go forward initially, and then bear left, now on a less distinct path along the edge of spoil.

A short way further on, you reach a large reedy area. Keep left around this, using a trackbed formed from slate scree. On the far side, as you head towards the main quarry, keep an eye open for a grassy path branching left from a modest cairn **C**. Follow the path easily across the moor to a col between Moelwyn Mawr and the isolated summit of Moel yr Hydd, which strong walkers might consider including in the walk. The path leads to a fence and gate **D**.

Through the gate, turn right and follow what turns out to be a delightful contouring terrace path across the flanks of Moelwyn Mawr and above

Llyn Cwmorthin lilies

Llyn Stwlan, which now comes into view. The traverse is superb, and should be followed all the way to Bwlch Stwlan, below the crags of Moelwyn Bach. At Bwlch Stwlan, marked by a large cairn and from which there is a fine view northwards of Moel Hebog above Beddgelert, about face and start descending a grassy ramp towards Llyn Stwlan, in effect doubling back beneath the path you have just walked. After about 50 yds, branch right on a less pronounced path descending between widespread boulders to the edge of a wide marshy area above the reservoir.

The path although wet is clear throughout and leads out to the southern end of the dam wall E, where steps take you down to a small patch of rough ground, crossing to a waymark ahead. At the waymark, cross a low wall and descend very steeply with care to a stile giving onto the dam service road a short distance ahead. Turn right down this and follow its zigzags, which gradually unravel, leaving you to stride onward all the way back to Tanygrisiau, reached at the bridge near the start of the walk. ●

walk 15

Tryfan

Start
Ogwen valley

Distance
3 miles (4.8km)

Height gain
1,755 feet (535m)

Approximate time
3½ hours

Route terrain
Rock and rocky paths throughout

Parking
Along A5, ½ mile east of Ogwen Cottage, on the southern shore of Llyn Ogwen

OS maps
Landranger 115 (Snowdon/Yr Wyddfa), Explorer OL17 (Snowdon/Yr Wyddfa)

GPS waypoints
SH 659 602
Ⓐ SH 664 600
Ⓑ SH 664 594
Ⓒ SH 661 588

Tryfan is not a mountain that can easily be ignored. By whichever approach along the A5, it rather captures your attention, and dramatically so. Even from more distant views, its crenulated outline stands buttressed against the Glyders, refusing to be left out. On a warm summer's day the feel of rock beneath fingertips as you thread your way through Tryfan's myriad ways is a happiness beyond compare.

⚠️ A strenuous walk with lots of rockwork and bouldery terrain; best saved for a fine day when route finding is less problematic. Do not rely too heavily on GPS waypoints; on this ascent they can only ever be approximate.

Start from a parking area along the A5, and go through a metal kissing-gate at the eastern end to pick your way through a jumble of boulders, then climbing steadily below the prominent rock climbing arena of Milestone Buttress, finally to reach a ladder-stile over a wall.

Beyond the wall, a well-trodden path ascends steeply for a while, initially across loose and broken ground until it arrives at a rock- and heather-covered shoulder. This is where you start on the North Ridge proper.

Walkers who are competent on rock may require little in the way of description. Those less comfortable need not fear, however, that Tryfan is barred to them, although it is fair to say that the ascent is unlikely to be accomplished with hands in pockets! Nor is that an invitation to try.

At the heathery shoulder, turn your attention to the ridge, although it resembles an impenetrable barrier of rock from this angle. But after a brief skirmish with scree, a way through does evolve, and is marked by countless thousands of feet. The route, as a result, is eroded in places, and is difficult in winter conditions, when an altogether different level of experience is called for. Generally, stick to the centre of the ridge, and soon you will arrive at a small platform with a large cairn known, since it is the meeting point of a number of routes (the Heather Terrace departs from here), as Piccadilly Circus Ⓐ.

Continue directly upwards and eventually the path arrives at a small, quartz-covered plateau to the right of which stands a finger of rock known as The Cannon, a feature you can actually pick out from the car park below.

A path to the left at this point leads upwards to another small plateau and a rock wall at the base of which there is a tumble of

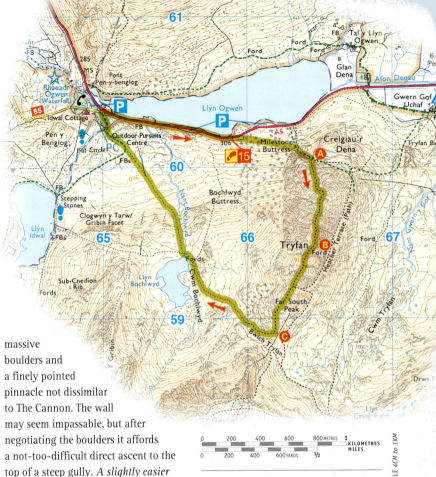

massive
boulders and
a finely pointed
pinnacle not dissimilar
to The Cannon. The wall
may seem impassable, but after
negotiating the boulders it affords
a not-too-difficult direct ascent to the
top of a steep gully. *A slightly easier
way bears left before tackling the
boulders, through a small gap just
before the wall, making a short descent
and re-ascent on an obvious path that
leads round a corner into the gully
itself. A scramble over blocks, including
a few awkward limb movements, takes
you to the top of the gully.*

Now a short scramble upwards leads
across a more level array of boulders to
a short rock descent to the top of
another, this time wider, gully. Then,
one final pull around the Central
Buttress sees you clambering to the top
of the mountain **B**.

Reaching the summit is one thing.
Getting back to Ogwen is another, and
best accomplished by heading down the
South Ridge, itself not without a few
awkward moments. But it is

Tryfan

The summit of Tryfan is
crowned by two huge
boulders known as Adam and Eve
(although which is which has never
really been clear). Many years ago,
the practice evolved of somehow
getting yourself onto the top of one
of the boulders and 'stepping' from
one to the other. This is not
recommended. Common sense
suggests that you simply reach up
and pat the top with your hand, at
least some part of you will have
conquered Tryfan.

considerably shorter, and the popular
way has become etched in the rocks:
the key is to avoid descending away
from the spine of the ridge too soon.
What you should be aiming to do is
head for the narrow neck of land, Bwlch

Tryfan

Tryfan ©, linking the mountain with the Glyders beyond. This is crossed by a wall and two ladder-stiles, and from here a clear path descends towards Llyn Bochlwyd.

But before you reach the actual bwlch, you can bear right and follow a clear path in a north-westerly direction down to the shores of the lake, a good place to relax and appreciate what you have done. Beyond the lake, the path drops more steeply, and leads down to Ogwen Cottage, from where you have to

walk back eastwards along the road to reach the starting point – this is the measured route.

There is a variant finish: Just as the path starts to descend from the lake, you will notice a prominent rock buttress on the right: this is Bochlwyd Buttress. Cross the stream flowing from Llyn Bochlwyd, and pass well below the Buttress following a sometimes tenuous path across boggy and bouldery terrain to return more directly to the car park. ●

Moel Hebog

Moel Hebog quite forcefully dominates Beddgelert, and its conquest, although straightforward in terms of route finding, is demanding. For this reason, the route is given here as an up-and-down walk, although this in no way detracts from its appeal. The mountain was certainly popular in Victorian times, when visitors would flock here for the view from its summit, although there is no record of how many didn't make it. Engage low gear; be prepared for a steady plod, uphill all the way, but then enjoy the summit at leisure.

There are a few places in Beddgelert to park, so begin from the main bridge spanning the Afon Colwyn, heading along the A4085 towards Caernarfon. Pass several inns, tearooms and an outdoors shop, and soon arrive at a turning on the left (signed 'Private Road'). Go this way, it is a public bridleway. Follow the track to pass beneath the restored Welsh Highland Railway line, past a couple of farmhouses and through woods to reach a barn Ⓐ in Cwm Cloch.

Welsh Highland Railway

The original Welsh Highland Railway opened in 1923, formed by merging older railways. It had uncertain developmental history, but was pushed along following the First World War mainly as a means to offset chronic unemployment. However, it was never a viable concern and a Receiver was appointed in 1927, and the line closed ten years later, and much of the track lifted in the 1940s. It was a huge white elephant of Welsh industrial history.

But then came happier times when a group of enthusiasts formed the Welsh Highland Railway Society in 1961, and restoration finally began in the 1970s. But many years were still to pass before the line linked Caernarfon and Rhyd Ddu. By 2010, the line was complete all the way to Porthmadog.

Immediately after the barn go through a gate, and follow the on-going path, which is well-defined and has route markers at intervals lower down. The initial ascent is easy enough, but a short distance farther on, the climbing begins in earnest, a steep and energetic haul all the way to the top of the mountain.

The path continues up an ill-defined ridge and swings to the left, below the spectacular crags of Y Diffwys, after which there

---

Start
Beddgelert

Distance
4¾ miles (7.4km)

Height gain
2,480 feet (755m)

Approximate time
3½ hours

Route terrain
Rugged mountain path; rough upland pastures

Parking
In Beddgelert

OS maps
Landranger 115 (Snowdon/Yr Wyddfa), Explorer OL17 (Snowdon/Yr Wyddfa)

GPS waypoints
SH 590 481
Ⓐ SH 580 479
Ⓑ SH 565 469

Moel Hebog

is some mild scrambling, and while this can be avoided, it is probably easier to deal with it. To take your mind off the effort, there is some interesting geology during the ascent including lava flows, pyroclastic 'bombs' and volcanic ash.

Higher up, the path becomes rocky and the route is marked by small cairns that lead a way up through the crags to a grassy shoulder, a false summit from below, which in turn leads to another short rocky stretch and the summit plateau.

The summit of Moel Hebog **B** is marked by a trig pillar near a stone wall, the only shelter hereabouts. The view, not surprisingly, is extensive, dominated to the north-east by the Snowdon massif, to the south-east by the tumble of mountains around Cnicht and the Moelwyns. Immediately to the north are a couple of lower summits, Moel yr Ogof and Moel Lefn, that are often combined by strong walkers into

a longer circuit. Beyond these, Cwm Pennant lies to the left (Walk 2), while directly ahead the sumptuous Nantlle Ridge undulates magnificently along the skyline.

For this walk, the return route simply reverses the ascent, and calls for just as much attention on the upper rocky stretch. ●

SCALE 1:25000 or 2½ INCHES to 1 MILE 4CM to 1KM

walk 17

Drum and Llyn Anafon

The Carneddau have a reputation for navigational confusion among those who walk their many rounded and often featureless summits; altitude and remoteness serve only to make matters worse. On this walk, no such difficulties are likely to arise, unless you persist in being inattentive. A good track leads all the way to the top of Drum (pronounced Drim), and back out from Llyn Anafon. Between these two points lies a steep and rough descent on a mix of grass, heather and rocky rubble. But it is quite short-lived, and should present no difficulty for careful walkers.

Leave the car park, and pass through a nearby gate, onto a stony track that soon swings left and climbs easily to meet a wall. Continue beside the wall for a short distance farther to reach overhead powerlines, where the track forks, the main track now bearing right (east) Ⓐ.

Stay along the main track, with the

The summit of Drum

grassy slopes of Foel Dduarth and Foel Ganol rising on the right, and an inspiring sweep of rough pasture flowing down to the Menai coast. There is a lovely view across the Traeth Lafan, too, to the eastern tip of Anglesey and Puffin Island. To the east rises the massive bulk of Tal y Fan, something of an outlier among these eastern mountains, but with a splendid prehistory of standing stones, burial chambers and ancient settlements.

The track, described on maps as a Roman Road, makes a fabulous traverse of the moorland, heading ultimately for Bwlch y Ddeufaen, and without significant ascent. Wander easily along the track until just after crossing a ridge descending northwards from Yr Orsedd, the track divides at a signpost **B**. Here, branch right for Drum, and climb more steeply across a landscape frequented by feral ponies and lushly carpeted in season with bilberries and heather.

The track you are following is a treasure, rising at an agreeable angle and

Llyn Anafon and wild ponies

Drum The summit of Drum goes by the name Carnedd Penydorth Goch, a title that hints at more than what is immediately evident. This is the site of a Bronze Age platform, roughly circular and about 60ft (18m) in diameter, with a marked terrace on the east side. The modern cairn-shelter is slightly west of the centre.

leading directly to the top of Drum **C**, a summit crowned by a large stone shelter, and enjoying an excellent view across Anglesey to far-away Holyhead Mountain. This is the point of return, but worthy of time spent relaxing and taking in the views.

Now comes the most awkward section, although it is perfectly acceptable to go back down the way you came up. Otherwise you need to strike off roughly in a westerly direction, down steepening slopes that drain to Llyn Anafon, a lonely lake that soon comes into view. Take both care and time as you descend, and, as you get your bearing, aim for the outflow of the lake, and avoid the marshy ground that surrounds it as much as possible.

A broad service track appears, and this is your target **D**. Once it is safely underfoot, all that remains is to amble out along the valley until you intercept the track used on the ascent at **A**, and then retrace your steps.

On the Cantilever
Glyder Fach

walk 18

Pont Scethin

Start
Dyffryn Ardudwy

Distance
8 miles (12.6km)

Height gain
1,295 feet (395m)

Approximate time
4½ hours

Route terrain
Moorland; upland tracks, some marshy ground, woodland

Parking
Village car park at start

OS maps
Landranger 124 (Porthmadog & Dolgellau), Explorer OL18 (Harlech, Porthmadog and Bala/y Bala)

GPS waypoints
⚐ SH 586 232
Ⓐ SH 588 232
Ⓑ SH 594 227
Ⓒ SH 634 235
Ⓓ SH 607 225
Ⓔ SH 597 222
Ⓕ SH 591 221
Ⓖ SH 589 225

For those who want to enjoy a long walk in open, wild, remote surroundings, but without strenuous ascents or challenging and difficult paths, this route in the southern Rhinogs (Rhinogydd in Welsh) is ideal. The going is easy throughout, the paths are clear and firm – apart from a few boggy sections in the middle part of the walk – and the scenery is superb. Near the end are three additional bonuses: delightful woodland, fine coastal views and two prehistoric burial chambers.

⚐ From the car park turn left up to the main road, cross over and take the uphill lane opposite, turning right at a junction, at a public footpath sign, along a track Ⓐ. This track soon meets with a tarred lane. Go ahead and left along this, following it as it becomes the access road to Tyddyn Du Farm. Just before reaching the farm turn right at a footpath sign, pass through two gates in quick succession, continue through a third and then bear slightly left along a walled, grassy track. After about 250yds, the walls splay apart at a gorsy knoll. Turn right

here along the right-hand edge of a field, by a wall and line of trees on the right, passing through a kissing-gate and continuing along the left-hand edge of the next field, this time with the wall on the left, to climb a ladder-stile on to a lane **B**.

Turn left along this lane, passing through an impressive avenue of trees, once part of the drive of Cors y Gedol Hall, curving right and left around the boundary wall of the hall and then turning right to continue in the same direction as before. Ahead are fine views of the southern Rhinogs, Y Llethr (Walk 28) and Diffwys in particular. Where the lane ends go through a gate, where a notice says 'No vehicles beyond this gate' and keep ahead along a broad, walled track, passing through a series of gates to continue through the wild,

open, lonely and barren terrain of the valley of the Afon Ysgethin. Pass through a final gate and wind with the moorland road easily uphill for about a quarter of a mile. At a left-hand bend (waymark pole), and below the middle of the plantation on the flanks of Moelfre off to your left, fork right along a grassy track. This strikes straight down across the moor to Pont Scethin, visible in the hollow below **C**.

This old packhorse bridge was once used by drovers on their way to England and, although it is difficult to believe it of such a remote spot, it was later used by mail coaches travelling between London and Harlech. Cross the bridge and follow the waymarked,

SCALE 1:25000 or 2½ INCHES to 1 MILE 4CM to 1KM

slabbed path gently uphill to reach an upright stone. Here turn right along an established green track. Remain with this for 2 miles, passing above lonely Llyn Erddyn, huddled beneath the striking face of Llawlech, and through a series of gates to reach a T-junction. Here turn right, passing through a gate to join a lane that curves right across Pont Fadog, another graceful old packhorse bridge over the Afon Ysgethin **D**.

Walk up to the cottage ahead. On the left, a bridleway runs into the woods of Coed Cors-y-gedol. This well-used path drops gradually through marvellous ancient oak woods, in places coming close to the tumbling river. Pass through a hand-gate and ignore two paths forking off to the right within the next 500yds. The path then rises gradually above the river to reach a bench and a fork **E**.

Keep right here, shortly keeping right again at a junction, joining a walled path through the trees. Near the edge of the woods keep left at a fork, soon crossing a bridge to gain a hand-gate raised on steps. With glorious views ahead across Cardigan Bay to the Lleyn Peninsula, join the tarred lane and walk downhill for just over a quarter of a mile. Immediately before reaching houses on the left, take the waymarked, high step-stile on the right **F**. Climb it and bear right to a metal gate and yellow waymark a few yards ahead on the left. Go through the gate and up steps across a very broad wall, go down steps on the other side and continue along the edge of a field, by a wall on the left. Climb more steps over another broad wall and continue along the right-hand edge of the next field, now with the wall on the right, passing through a metal gate. Bear right to join a farm track and follow it through several gates down to a lane **G**.

Cross over, go through the gate opposite and bear right across a field towards its top edge. Continue along the edge of the field, by a wall on the right,

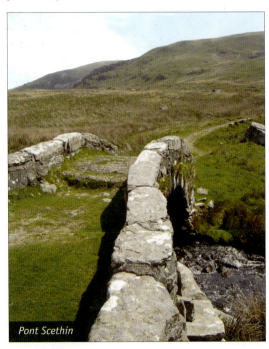

Pont Scethin

climb a stone stile to enter woodland, walk through the wood and at the far end keep ahead across a field, bearing left to pass through a hand-gate. Now continue by a wall on the left – the boundary wall of the Dyffryn Burial Chambers, which date from the Neolithic period. Keep ahead past the burial chambers, on an enclosed path beside a school to reach the main road. Turn right and walk through the village back to the car park. ●

Cnicht

walk 19

Start
Croesor

Distance
6¾ miles (10.7km)

Height gain
1,950 feet (595m)

Approximate time
4½ hours

Route terrain
Rough mountain upland; steep slopes; remnant quarry tracks

Parking
National Park car park (Pay and Display) at Croesor

OS maps
Landrangers 115 (Snowdon/Yr Wyddfa) and 124 (Porthmadog & Dolgellau), Explorers OL17 (Snowdon/Yr Wyddfa) and OL18 (Harlech, Porthmadog & Bala/y Bala)

GPS waypoints
SH 631 446
Ⓐ SH 628 450
Ⓑ SH 645 466
Ⓒ SH 657 478
Ⓓ SH 665 462
Ⓔ SH 636 449

Rising to 2,265ft (690m), Cnicht is possibly the most distinctive of all the Snowdonia peaks. The ascent from Croesor is rewarding and challenging, a deceptively easy initial section culminating in a steep scramble to gain the summit. From here, springy turf paths fall towards remote Llyn yr Adar, thence via evocative slate-quarrying remains to a descent along the flank of Cwm Croesor.

⚠️This walk is best done on a fine day, both for the remarkable views and to allow line-of-sight navigation near Llyn Cwm-corsiog. Some sections will be slippery underfoot in wet or cold weather. There are steep slopes near the summit. Between Ⓒ and Ⓓ the route may be boggy, and is easy to lose.

Turn right out of the car park and walk through the village, passing a chapel on the right and continuing along the uphill tarmac track ahead. Continue to a ladder-stile, climb it and keep ahead along a rough track that heads up through woodland.

Just beyond the woods bear right, passing through a waymarked open gateway Ⓐ on a broad, stony track which initially continues uphill but soon flattens out. From now on the distinctive, pointed shape of Cnicht is in sight most of the time.

Climb a ladder-stile beside a metal gate and continue through an increasingly wild and rocky landscape. The track, now a grassy path, rises gently to a ruinous sheepfold; here turn right (waymarked) below a low crag then bear left up to a ladder-stile. Climb this and turn left, continuing the easy ascent towards the still-distant summit.

On meeting a wall, keep it on your right to find and climb a wooden step-stile. Turn left beside the wall, then shortly fork right along a narrow path beneath the snout of a crag. Cross a grassy area to find a cairn, beyond which keep ahead up a steepening, faint path to gain another grassy plateau. Again walk to its far end, in line with the summit. Pass right of the cairn and along a thin, level path below a rock face, shortly commencing a testing four-limb scramble up a narrow, steep, braided path that spreads to the summit; if in doubt favour your left hand. This challenging approach above steep drops gains the bristly summit rocks Ⓑ, from which modest top are fabulous views to the Glyders, Snowdon, Moel Hebog, Cardigan

The final pull onto Cnicht

Bay and the Lleyn Peninsula.

Continue north-east from the summit along an obvious path, keep right of the second sub-summit to a small pond then go ahead left along a wide grassy swathe, aiming for the conical peak of distant Moel Siabod. A distinct path soon forms, tracing a low ridge high above Llyn Biswail, eventually emerging 200yds above the remote Llyn yr Adar, off to your left. The low ridge erupts into squat rocky outcrops, between the lowest of which is a large cairn **C**.

Turn right here; follow the narrow path to cross a stream, then walk to a low rise and a second, small cairn. The path, not always as clear as might be liked, winds half-left, dropping down into a shallow valley. You should aim to rise to the pillow-like rocks on the next low ridge. From here, look ahead to the upper lake *(N.B. not the twin Diffwys lakes, to which you might be drawn)* and pick a way down into and across the marshy hollow, rising again to a low ridge before dropping towards the shore of Llyn Cwm-corsiog.

Walk along the right-hand bank to a metal kissing-gate just above one of the impounding dams. Go through this and walk parallel to the wire fence (right) before angling left to reach the atmospheric ruins **D** of Rhosydd slate mine buildings. Facing the front of the tumbled cottages turn right to find and follow the trackbed of an old railway beyond a gate and slate shed.

Curve left with this, a stream emerging down to your left. You need to drop to this before reaching a high embankment where the trackbed loops right; the easiest place is after the

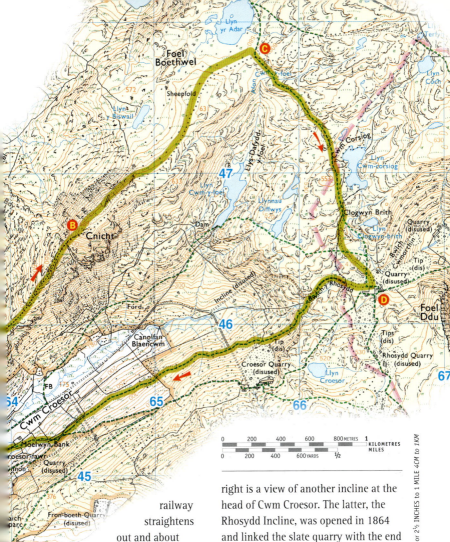

SCALE 1:25 000 or 2½ INCHES to 1 MILE 4CM to 1KM

railway straightens out and about 80yds before the embankment. Trace this stream (left) to a point opposite the far end of the wall beyond the water. Carefully cross here to pick up a thin path down across scree, the stream tumbling over a waterfall behind and to your right. This path soon establishes itself as a wide track that gradually descends this low northern flank of Moelwyn Mawr above Cwm Croesor, a superb glaciated valley. There are splendid views down the valley towards the Hebogs with Cnicht standing out prominently on the right. Go through a wooden gate and continue, crossing an incline. To the right is a view of another incline at the head of Cwm Croesor. The latter, the Rhosydd Incline, was opened in 1864 and linked the slate quarry with the end of the Croesor Tramway. Worked by gravity, the tramway carried slates from the local quarries to Porthmadog. Now the track continues as a pleasant, grassy ledge, descending gently, later keeping by a wire fence on the right and crossing another incline.

Climb a ladder-stile beside a gate and head downhill on a rough track towards the farm buildings. Climb another ladder-stile and keep left along the rough lane, which soon becomes tarred **E**. Remain on this, passing a convenient **café**, to Croesor, turning right at the crossroads to return to the car park. ●

Carnedd Llywelyn

Carnedd Llywelyn is the highest of the Carneddau. The line of ascent is straightforward and for much of the way follows a reservoir service road. But once beyond this, you fall into the clutch of craggy, high mountain walking of the most excellent kind.

⚠ The summit of Carnedd Llywelyn is a massive boulder and stone field that has considerable potential for navigational confusion. For this reason, the ascent of this fine mountain should be reserved for a clear and settled day.

Just a short distance to the east, along the A5, from the entrance to Gwern Gof Isaf farm, a gate gives onto a rising service track that spurs you all the way up to Ffynnon Llugwy Reservoir, in the shadow of the mighty whaleback of Pen yr Helgi du. As the track swings to the left towards the reservoir, you should leave it Ⓐ to cross a moderately damp stretch of ground, and locate a rising path that climbs through rocks and rough ground to the narrow neck of land, the Saddle, between Carnedd Llywelyn and Pen yr Helgi Du that rejoices in the name Bwlch Eryl Farchog Ⓑ. Make a mental note of the point

The way up onto Carnedd Llywelyn

at which the upwards path joins the Saddle; you will need it on the way back.

This is a narrow place, so there is little scope for confusion. Across the bwlch, the land falls sharply into Cwm Eigiau, a breathtaking view that will slip in and out of much of the walk from now on.

From the bwlch, follow a clear path upwards, in a north-westerly direction. It starts by threading a way through a brief rocky hiatus, where frequent pause for thought will bring a solution to route finding easier than brash assault. Once above this, the cliffs of Craig yr Ysfa are off to the right, a splendid rock gymnasts' playground,

SCALE 1:25000 or 2½ INCHES to 1 MILE 4CM to 1KM

Looking down on Bwlch Eryl Farchog (The Saddle)

with fine views down into Cwm Eigiau.

The gradient eases now, as a clear path presses ever upwards, zigzagging a little to ease the climb, but finally pulling up to the huge cairn on the top of Llywelyn.

The summit can be a bleak place, and because it is above surrounding

Carnedd Llywelyn Carnedd Llywelyn is the highest of this huge range of mountains, which seems to ripple away in all directions. It is a widely held view that the mountain was named after Llywelyn ap Gruffudd ap Llywelyn (c1223-1282), the last independent Prince of Wales.

mountains, the various ways off cannot be seen. So, keep your line of ascent clearly in mind if you intend to explore - it's the way you will be going down.

Leave the summit by retracing your steps back to Craig yr Ysfa, followed by a little rocky scrambling as you head down to Bwlch Eryl Farchog. Be sure to correctly locate the top of the path rising from Fynnon Llugwy Reservoir; it is clear enough, but is the only sensible way down from this point. Initially, it is steep, but then eases lower down as you press on to rejoin the reservoir service road, and follow this down to the A5, now with fine views across the valley to Tryfan and the Glyders. ●

Gwydyr Forest and the Swallow Falls

This superb walk provides outstanding views, and passes through a great variety of scenery and terrain. An initial steady climb out of the Llugwy valley through the conifers of Gwydyr Forest leads to a fine viewpoint overlooking Llyn Elsi, and is followed by a descent into the Llugwy gorge at the Miners' Bridge. The walk then proceeds up the beautifully wooded gorge to the Ugly House. Then the highlight of the walk is a 2½-mile ramble beside or above the River Llugwy, passing the spectacular Swallow Falls and finally crossing riverside meadows to Betws-y-coed – undoubtedly one of the most attractive riverside walks in the country.

Start	Betws-y-coed
Distance	8½ miles (13.5km)
Height gain	1,625 feet (495m)
Approximate time	5 hours
Route terrain	Woodland; riverside paths; road walking
Parking	Car park at edge of village
OS maps	Landranger 115 (Snowdon/Yr Wyddfa), Explorer OL17 (Snowdon/Yr Wyddfa)

GPS waypoints

- SH 795 565
- Ⓐ SH 788 566
- Ⓑ SH 784 555
- Ⓒ SH 771 557
- Ⓓ SH 779 569
- Ⓔ SH 771 575
- Ⓕ SH 756 575
- Ⓖ SH 772 577

Betws-y-coed With its dramatic location at the junction of three narrow, wooded valleys (Conwy, Llugwy and Lledr), it is easy to see why Betws-y-coed developed into a major tourist and walking centre. The simple 14th-century church tucked away near the railway station possesses an effigy of Gruffydd ap Dafydd, nephew of Llywelyn, last native prince of Wales. In 1873, the church was superseded by the handsome Victorian Gothic structure in the village centre. Some interesting bridges span the rivers, including the 18th-century stone Pont-y-pair ('Bridge of the Cauldron'), a suspension footbridge, and Telford's celebrated Waterloo Bridge. For rainy days there is a comprehensive information centre, railway museum, motor museum and RSPB centre.

From the car park by the station cross a grassy area to the Victorian church and turn right along the main road. After about a quarter of a mile look out for waymarked steps Ⓐ on the left behind a bus stop, just past 'The Pottery', which mark the start of the Jubilee Path waymarked by green paint blobs. Go up the steps onto a steep, zigzag path through trees and bushes to reach a track. Turn left for a few strides and then strike sharp right along a narrow path through dense woodland. Although most of the first part of this walk is through conifers, the route is fairly easy to follow because of the many green waymarks painted on rocks.

Continue uphill, the path marked by occasional yellow waymark arrows and faded green blobs. Cross straight over a forestry road and continue climbing. After about 300yds pass through a broken wall, beyond which the path becomes well

graded and virtually level, still in the forest. On reaching a curving forestry road at the edge of the trees, go straight across to join an undulating, slate path leading to the Ancaster Monument **B**. From here are lovely views across Llyn Elsi Reservoir to the Glyders, the Carneddau and shapely Siabod.

Turn sharp right from the monument on the gravelled path marked by a white-topped post. Drop down this to reach a footbridge immediately below a small dam. Turn right just before this to find a car parking area beside a forestry road. Turn left along this road, descending gradually and passing well above the remote 'Hafodlas' cottage. At the T-junction sweep right on the main drag, rising gently to pastures high in the forest.

Take the second track to the left, through a wooden gate guarding the access road to 'Pant-yr-hyddod'. A short distance before the farmhouse, fork to the right, climbing a wall-side path to the right of the grounds. Go through a kissing-gate and directly ahead, rising through bracken on a grassy path (occasionally waymarked), walking through to a wide grassy track by a woodland edge fence. Bear right alongside this, ignore the first gate on your left and drop to a metal walker's gate beside a field gate **C**.

Once through the gate, keep ahead at the immediate junction and pass by a ruin, part of the now largely deserted former mining village of Rhiwddolion. Shortly after passing by a cottage on your left, you'll reach a crossways; here your way is ahead and through two near-spaced wooden gates (marked with blue blobs), joining a rough track heading down into the woods. This is the route of the Roman Road of Sarn Helen, named after the Welsh-born wife of the 4th-century Emperor Magnus

Maximus. Pass by another cottage, just beyond which go straight across a track and down a path that drops over a footbridge and then through two gates to gain a tarred lane leading to the A5 road. Cross straight over into the entrance opposite and go ahead towards the Miners' Bridge **D**.

Anyone wishing to follow a shorter walk should descend to and climb the bridge and turn immediately right to join the (initially very narrow) path back to Betws-y-coed. This reduces the overall distance to 5 miles (8km).

Turn left just before the Miners' Bridge onto a path that undulates gently through the woods clothing the Llugwy Gorge. This is part of the Artist's Wood Walk, its name recalling the area's popularity with Victorian painters. Occasionally awkward underfoot, the path reaches a ruined mine building; here turn left up to the A5 **E**.

Turn right and walk the roadside tarred footpath for 1¼ miles, en route passing the **Swallow Falls Hotel**. Cross the river bridge, beyond which is Ty-hyll ('The Ugly House'), named after the irregular, rough blocks of its construction, which allegedly took just one day.

Take the steps and a ladder-stile on the right at the end of the bridge **F**, joining a riverside path beside meadows. Two further ladder-stiles find you in woodland on a braided path

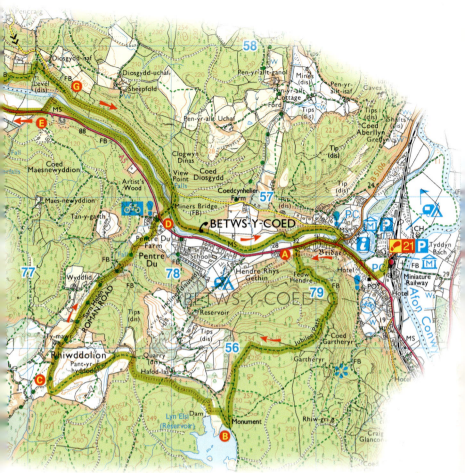

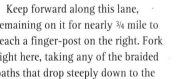

SCALE 1:25000 or 2½ INCHES to 1 MILE 4CM to 1KM

rising gradually left above the river. Join the wide forest path and turn right, guided by yellow-topped posts. In 200yds, keep right at a fork, soon passing another post. The path narrows to a fenced ledge; shortly steps to the right access a viewing platform above the Swallow Falls.

Rejoin the path and continue downstream, keeping right at a fork for Betws-y-coed. Cross a footbridge and rise to join a track. Bear right; shortly keep right as a track comes in sharply from the left and then in 25 paces fork left up a narrower path marked by yellow flashes on trees. Pass through a broken wall and rise to an isolated footpath finger-post. Keep right, cross a footbridge and trace the main path up to join a lane **G**.

Keep forward along this lane, remaining on it for nearly ¾ mile to reach a finger-post on the right. Fork right here, taking any of the braided paths that drop steeply down to the Miners' Bridge, a wooden bridge built at a steep, almost 45° tilt which was once used by local miners to get to and from work. Do not cross it but turn left to follow a wooded riverside path.

Soon after climbing a ladder-stile continue across meadows dotted with trees, climb a stile and pass through more woodland to reach the stone arches of Pont-y-pair. Turn right over the bridge and turn left along the road to return to the starting point. ●

Start
Beddgelert

Distance
8½ miles (13.3km)

Height gain
1,770 feet (540m)

Approximate time
5 hours

Route terrain
Rugged upland trails; woodland; lane walking; riverside path

Parking
In Beddgelert

OS maps
Landranger 115 (Snowdon/Yr Wyddfa), Explorer OL17 (Snowdon/Yr Wyddfa)

GPS waypoints
- ✏ SH 590 481
- Ⓐ SH 604 488
- Ⓑ SH 619 493
- Ⓒ SH 635 490
- Ⓓ SH 629 479
- Ⓔ SH 613 465
- Ⓕ SH 606 461
- Ⓖ SH 601 460
- Ⓗ SH 597 461
- Ⓙ SH 594 462
- Ⓚ SH 591 473

Nanmor valley and Aberglaslyn

This splendid walk through a majestic landscape provides outstanding views and scenic variety without any strenuous climbing or difficult terrain. From Beddgelert a pleasant and easy route, initially by the Afon Glaslyn and later along the shores of Llyn Dinas, is followed by a gradual ascent to the head of the Nanmor valley. The route, much of it through delightful woodland, then descends equally gently to Nantmor and on to Pont Aberglaslyn before the highlight of the walk – through the awe-inspiring Pass of Aberglaslyn.

Beddgelert

Situated at the meeting of the Glaslyn and Colwyn rivers, and surrounded by some of the highest mountains in Snowdonia, Beddgelert is an excellent walking centre with a range of cafés, hotels, pubs and restaurants.

Visitors are drawn here as much by the legend of Gelert as by its location. The story of the faithful dog Gelert, killed by its master, Prince Llywelyn, who wrongly thought that the dog had killed his baby son when in fact it had saved the child by killing a wolf, seems to have been a highly successful piece of publicity created by the landlord of the Royal Goat Inn in 1801. It was he who erected the cairn which is supposed to mark the dog's grave and which is now a major tourist attraction. Near the meeting of the rivers is a 13th-century church, on the site of an earlier Celtic monastery associated with St Celert, the latter more likely than the legendary hound to be the origin of the name of the village.

✏ Start from the village centre bridge, by taking the tarred lane signed for Gelert's Grave, walking downstream with the Afon Colwyn on your left. Cross the footbridge at the confluence of the Glaslyn and Colwyn, bear left beside the village green and walk through to a lane. Cross straight over, continuing upstream on the waymarked footpath beside the Afon Glaslyn amidst copious growths of rhododendrons. Climb a ladder-stile into a tarred lane and bear right along it. This becomes a rough track beyond a gate; remain on this to reach the entrance to the Sygun Copper Mine. Abandoned in 1903, this is now a popular visitor attraction where an underground visit reveals the process of extraction and the lives led by Victorian miners.

Bear left at the entrance Ⓐ to a bridge over the Glaslyn. Do not cross this; rather join the waymarked footpath via a gate and walk the well-graded path above the river, use a hand-gate and continue to reach the foot of Llyn Dinas and a footbridge. Do not cross, but use the metal kissing-gate to join a lakeside path, ford a stream and walk round to a ladder-stile. Beyond this take the right-hand fork, leaving the lakeside route to rise behind a small wooded bluff – the view back along Nantgwynant is exceptional. Pass by the overgrown ruins of a cottage, dropping to a ladder-stile and views across Llyn Dinas. Climb the stile and keep right on a woodland edge path to reach a further ladder-stile Ⓑ on your right about 100yds beyond a plank bridge.

Aberglaslyn Pass

Climb the stile and trace the well-used path through the woods, passing a ruined cottage. Just above this, use the wall gap and turn sharp-left, beyond which the path steepens and winds uphill to a ladder-stile out of the woods. The path now undulates through craggy country offering lovely views of this heart of Snowdonia. Swing right off a low crag, shortly passing a waymark post and rising to the near end of a green bowl below low bluffs. Turn left here to climb a ladder-stile just beyond a plank bridge. Now turn right along the waymarked path, rising on a twisting route to another stile near the remote Hafod Owen cottage. Pass immediately left of the cottage, drop down to the ladder-stile and turn right, then left to put a wall on your left. Keep ahead on the obvious path as the wall fails, rising gently to a ladder-stile beside a stand of conifers. Keep the wall on your right, cross straight over the rough road and keep going to climb a ladder-stile on your right. Turn left beside the wall, rising steeply to a wall gap, beyond which bear half-left to another wall gap on a low mound. Head for the gate visible to the right of the cottage ahead, beside which is a tarred lane Ⓒ.

Turn right along this lane down the secluded and verdant Nanmor valley, passing by the remains of slate quarries to reach a bridge across the Afon Nanmor Ⓓ. Climb a ladder-stile on the right just before the bridge, joining a waymarked riverside path through superb oak woods. Leave the woods via another ladder-stile and walk in front of a cottage, following the path through reedy pasture, a wall gap and then across a bracken-covered slope to a hand-gate back into woods. The path rises gently beyond a metal gate, shortly crossing a ladder-stile beyond which it steepens through the woods, passing by a waymark post to pick up a wall on your left. Use the path passing above and behind the renovated cottage, continuing beyond on a wallside path. The path eventually

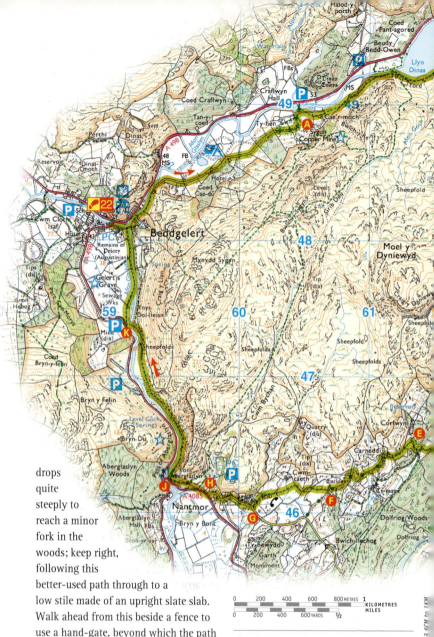

drops quite steeply to reach a minor fork in the woods; keep right, following this better-used path through to a low stile made of an upright slate slab. Walk ahead from this beside a fence to use a hand-gate, beyond which the path rises gradually above a large reedy meadow, briefly skirting the edge of the woods before dropping again to the edge of the meadow.

Near the end of the meadow, the path turns right across it to join a slate track beyond, climbing and winding steeply up to a pasture crossed by wooden pylons. Turn left at a footpath sign beneath these , passing through a

gate to join a partly slabbed path beside a wall. Go through a kissing-gate and rise along the field edge to use the right-hand one of two gates into a farmyard; walk through to the tarred lane and turn left down this. There are wonderful views from this twisting lane across to the mountains above Beddgelert and down to the coast and the Lleyn Peninsula. Remain on the lane

to reach the first house on your left **F**.

Look right here for a wall gap, drop down the few steps and walk ahead to pass between two trees mid-field to use a waymarked gap at a wall junction beyond. Look ahead left for a hand-gate beneath a tree, use this and go ahead across the reedy pasture. It's very boggy here, but persevere, aiming to pass just left of the low rocky outcrop to reach a gate beside the bungalow. Join the lane here, walking past houses to reach a junction beside Chapel Peniel here in Nantmor **G**.

Turn right and fall with the lane to a junction. En route you'll cross the course of the Welsh Highland Railway. Turn right along the main road for a short distance before forking right into the National Trust car park here at their Aberglaslyn Estate.

Turn left at the notice board and

toilet block **H**, crossing a stone stile onto a stony path that climbs easily into the woods. Rise to another path along which bear left to reach and use a hand-gate. The path braids; simply keep ahead, shortly passing immediately above an old cottage before dropping steeply beside a fence on your left to reach a roadside kissing-gate at Pont Aberglaslyn **J**.

It's worth walking onto the bridge for the superb view up the gorge. Return to the gate and join the narrow path above the river. This is the Fisherman's Path, an adventurous route up through the gorge that rises and falls across boulders, on ledges and a few short sections of suspended boardwalk above the rushing river. Soon after these boardwalks the path splits; take the left fork to continue beside the river. Up to your right is the entrance to an old railway tunnel. This is the route of the Welsh Highland Railway, a narrow gauge (1ft 11½ins) line between Porthmadog and Caernarfon, built both to carry tourists and to move slate to the ports at the two termini. It only operated between 1923 and 1937, but has recently been revived, and is now a popular attraction.

As the gorge fails, there are several opportunities to join the track bed, or simply remain on the riverside path. Cross the footbridge **K** over the Afon Glaslyn and turn right on the concrete path, following this all the way back into Beddgelert. You may divert to the left at a junction beside the river-gauge building to visit 'Gelert's Grave'. ●

Aran Benllyn

Start
Pont y Pandy,
Llanuwchllyn

Distance
7½ miles (12km)

Height gain
2,295 feet (700m)

Approximate time
5 hours

Route terrain
Farmland; mountain
upland

Parking
National Trust car park
at Pont y Pandy, on the
B4403 at Llanuwchllyn

OS maps
Landranger 125 (Bala
& Lake Vyrnwy/y Bala
a Llyn Efyrnwy),
Explorer OL23 (Cadair
Idris & Llyn Tegid)

GPS waypoints

  SH 879 297
Ⓐ SH 878 292
Ⓑ SH 875 287
Ⓒ SH 872 262
Ⓓ SH 868 246

Although neighbouring Aran Fawddwy is the higher of the two, it is Aran Benllyn that is visually better known, rising as it does from the southern end of Llyn Tegid (Bala Lake). This ascent to Benllyn is a straight up-and-down walk, but the incremental nature of the landscape, the way it undulates upwards, brings pleasure at every stride, concealing what lies ahead for much of the route. And while the amount of ascent may seem a little daunting, it all drops away easily enough, taking you high onto the mountain before you know it.

The walk begins from a small National Trust car park at Pont y Pandy, spanning the Afon Twrch, in the village of Llanuwchllyn to the south of Bala lake.

From the car park, head towards the bridge, but do not cross it; instead cross the road to a ladder-stile beside a gate. Follow a narrow lane beyond to a bridleway signpost and ladder-stile beside a gate Ⓐ. Ascend diagonally up-field following a shallow track to another stile, beyond which the continuing bridleway runs around the northern end of Garth Fach.

At the next gate and stile, continue following a sunken bridleway until it divides at a low waymark Ⓑ, and here bear left, climbing steadily to cross a wall, after which the path is now accompanied by a fence.

Aran Benllyn Known for a litany of false summits, so, tempting as it might be to suppose that you can see the mountain top ahead, you can't, and won't see it for some time. On the plus side, this lovely undulating characteristic actually makes the climb more agreeable as you tackle Moel Ddu, Craig y Geifr and Moel Ffenigl, all sufficiently pronounced minor tops to inject interest. A nearby fenceline is also a feature to be trusted, as it leads to the very summit of the mountain, and beyond. It doesn't quite touch upon the highest point of Benllyn, but it runs closely by, and is a sure guide in poor visibility.

The first stages of the ascent are easy, dropping quite early on through a dip to a stile at the end of a wall, after which the path starts to climb more energetically. To the east, by way of distraction, the rolling, lush, patterned pastures of Cwm Cynllwyd and its hill farms are a particular delight.

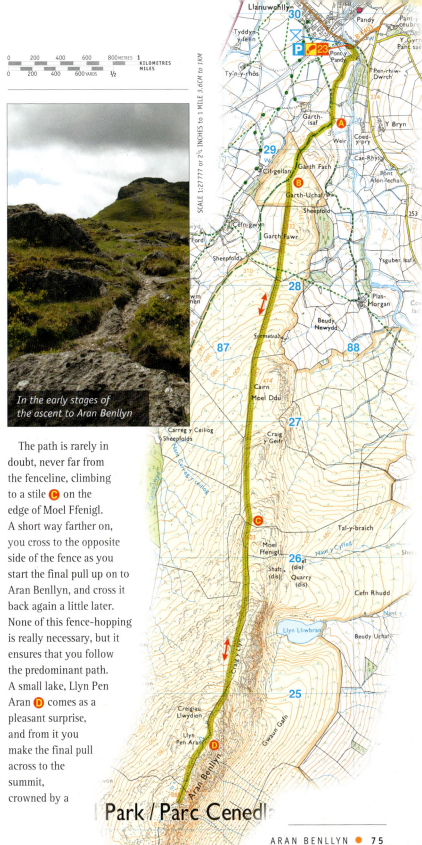

In the early stages of
the ascent to Aran Benllyn

The path is rarely in doubt, never far from the fenceline, climbing to a stile **C** on the edge of Moel Ffenigl. A short way farther on, you cross to the opposite side of the fence as you start the final pull up on to Aran Benllyn, and cross it back again a little later. None of this fence-hopping is really necessary, but it ensures that you follow the predominant path. A small lake, Llyn Pen Aran **D** comes as a pleasant surprise, and from it you make the final pull across to the summit, crowned by a

Park / Parc Cened

neat cairn of quartz.

The top of Aran Benllyn has a rash of rocky outcrops, and the makings of a wall, although the function of a wall hereabouts is vague. The view, as might be supposed, is quite splendid and embraces virtually all of the northern Snowdonian mountains rippling away into a far blue haze.

The simple act of retracing your steps to Pont y Pandy will conclude a splendid day, high among the Arans. ●

On the summit of Aran Benllyn, looking north to Rhobell Fawr and Snowdon

Moel Eilio

walk 24

Start
Llanberis

Distance
8 miles (13km)

Height gain
2,445 feet (745m)

Approximate time
5 hours

Route terrain
Mountain tracks;
grassy upland

Parking
In Llanberis

OS maps
Landranger 115
(Snowdon/Yr Wyddfa),
Explorer OL17
(Snowdon/Yr Wyddfa)

GPS waypoints
🔖 SH 580 601
Ⓐ SH 576 600
Ⓑ SH 566 596
Ⓒ SH 561 598
Ⓓ SH 556 577
Ⓔ SH 572 558
Ⓕ SH 572 590

Often overlooked in favour of higher fare elsewhere, Moel Eilio and its two acolytes, Foel Gron and Foel Goch, are the most splendid escapism. Springy turf cushions the feet, and fine, airy views please the eye. Throw in relative solitude, and the stage is set for one of the most enjoyable circuits in Snowdonia.

🔖 The route begins in Llanberis by walking up Ffordd Capel Goch – the road to the youth hostel, from the High Street. At Pen y Bont Ⓐ, turn right into Fron Goch, and then, at the top of a rise, swing left towards the Plas Garnedd Care Centre. Beyond the centre, a gated lane climbs through farmland dotted with derelict buildings. The final such building, Maen-llwyd-isaf, with Moel Eilio and the valley of the Afon Goch rising on the left, is where the lane surfacing ends and a rough track takes you upwards to a ladder-stile Ⓑ.

Once over the stile, bear left beside a wall. The track takes you past the site of Dinas Osian, an Iron Age settlement and hill fort, although there is little to see of it today. Continue to a gate across the track not far from the top of the ascent at Bwlch y Groes, and through the gate continue a little farther as far as a branching grassy vehicle track Ⓒ. Leave the Bwlch y Groes path here, and climb easily onto the long and broad northern ridge of Moel Eilio, which is a pleasure to walk. Soon, the track merges with one that has ascended from Bwlch y Groes. The path gives lovely views to the west of the Lleyn Peninsula and Yr Eifl (The Rivals), across Caernarfon and across the Menai Strait to Anglesey to Holyhead Mountain.

As you approach the top section of Moel Eilio, you encounter a fence. Walk alongside this, the path taking you finally to a ladder-stile not far from the summit. Over the stile, bear right beside the on-going fenceline and soon reach the large stone-built shelter on the summit Ⓓ. The view is expansive and inspiring, embracing the Nantlle Ridge and Mynydd Mawr in particular.

The continuation from Moel Eilio follows a fenceline descending steeply roughly in a south-easterly direction. Follow the fence down to a stile at a wall corner beyond which lie the twin summits of Foel Gron. From this summit there is a stunning view of Cwm Dwythwch and its lake, and then, after a dip, a final pull leads to a ladder-stile near a fence corner on Foel Goch. The summit is singularly undistinguished, other than by a tiny, low-lying cairn. But it does offer fine retrospective views of Moel Eilio.

Return to the ladder-stile, and then take to a narrow path descending very steeply to Bwlch Maesgwm **E**, a high mountain pass below bulky Moel Cynghorion. At the pass, turn left and descend a broad trail roughly northwards through the valley slopes of Foel Goch and Moel Cynghorion. As you descend, so the track drops steadily towards civilisation, finally reaching a lane head **F**.

Now simply turn down the lane, passing the youth hostel, and so make your way back to Llanberis.

SCALE 1:25 000 or 2½ INCHES to 1 MILE 4CM to 1KM

0	200	400	600	800 METRES	1	
					KILOMETRES	
					MILES	
0	200	400	600 YARDS	½		

Retrospective view of Moel Eilio and Foel Gron from Foel Goch

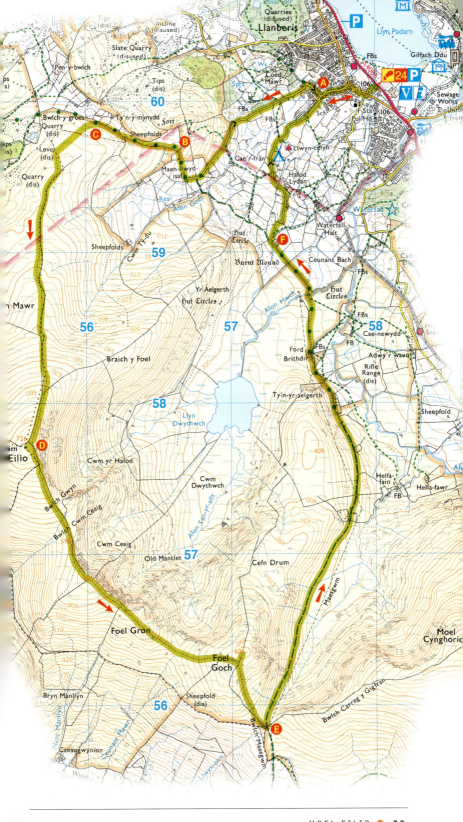

walk 25

Snowdon (Yr Wyddfa)

Sooner or later any serious walker in Snowdonia will want to tackle Yr Wyddfa – Snowdon itself – and it is a tremendously satisfying and exhilarating feeling to stand on the highest point in England and Wales, at 3,560ft (1,085m), surveying a magnificent panoramic view. This route uses the Pyg Track on the outward journey and the Miners' Track on the return, and is one of the easier of several alternatives: the starting point is over 1,100ft (335m), at the top of the Llanberis Pass, and the paths are well constructed and easy to follow.

⚠ Even so, it must be emphasised that this walk must be avoided in bad weather and mist, especially during the winter or whenever snow covers the higher ground, unless you are equipped for, and experienced in, mountain walking in these conditions.

Join the Pyg Track at the back-right corner of the upper car park. It's tarred for 50 paces before a gap stile leads to the path proper. This climbs to Bwlch y Moch, 'the Pass of the Pigs',

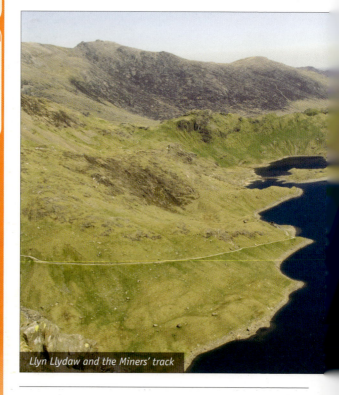

Llyn Llydaw and the Miners' track

a well-maintained path that climbs steadily, using steps in places, and bears left to reach Bwlch y Moch . Keep ahead below the towering slopes of Crib Goch, high above Llyn Llydaw. Ahead, the distinctive, pyramid-shaped summit of Snowdon now comes into view, although the twin-peaked summit, Y Lliwedd, shares equal billing for the moment.

The route, which twists and turns, makes a gradual ascent, probing ever farther into the upper confines of this vast cwm through which access seems to be barred by a massive headwall of rock. After passing the top of the path rising from the Miners' Track, which joins from the left , the path begins to climb more steeply, bearing right and heading up a series of zigzags – this is the most strenuous part of the walk – eventually reaching the track of the Snowdon Mountain Railway by a tall marker stone .

Snowdon Mountain Railway

The railway, a triumph of Victorian engineering in such terrain, is the only rack-and-pinion railway in Britain and was opened to passenger traffic in 1896. The journey from Llanberis to Snowdon's summit is about 5 miles (8km) with an average gradient of 1 in 7.

Turn left and walk uphill by the side of the track to the summit station – the actual summit of the mountain is just above it to the left , a trig pillar perched on a rocky plinth. The views from here, the highest point in Britain south of the Scottish Highlands, are magnificent; they extend over much of North Wales and in exceptionally clear conditions can include the Wicklow Mountains in Ireland, the Isle of Man and some of the higher Lake District peaks.

For the descent first retrace your steps to the junction of the Pyg and

Miners' tracks, taking care not to miss the tall stone **C**, where you turn right away from the railway track. At the junction of the tracks **B**, where there is a stone marker about 3 feet high, bear right and descend steeply, *with great care to the shores of Glaslyn – this is probably the most difficult section of the whole route, so be careful and take time.*

On reaching the lake follow the broad, fairly flat and well-constructed track along the shores of Glaslyn and then descending to Llyn Llydaw, passing some of the ruined buildings of the Britannia Copper Mine. These include the miners' barracks and the large building beside Llyn Llydaw which was the ore-crushing mill. Near the end of the lake follow the track to the right across the causeway **E**, built in 1853 to make it easier to transport copper from the mines above Glaslyn to Pen-y-pass. It is obvious why the track

is so broad, well-constructed and relatively flat. From the causeway there is a dramatic view of almost the whole of the Snowdon Horseshoe – from the ridge of Crib Goch around to Yr Wyddfa and along the cliffs of Y Lliwedd to Llyn Llydaw.

After crossing the causeway, the track bears to the left and for the final section of the walk is most attractive. The track continues above the little Llyn Teyrn, where there are more remains of miners' barracks, and from the track there is a final superb retrospective view of Snowdon.

Easing onwards, the track leads back to Pen-y-pass with yet more spectacular views: to the right looking down Nantgwynant and ahead to the impressive profiles of Moel Siabod and the Glyders. ●

SCALE 1:25000 or 2½ INCHES to 1 MILE 4CM to 1KM

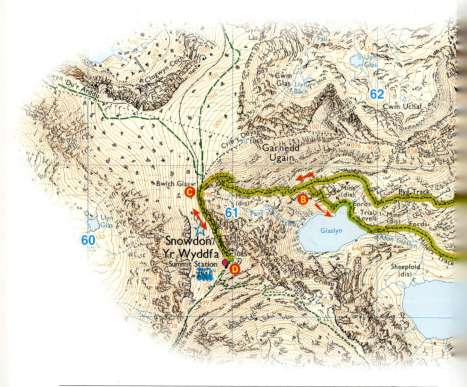

Summit memorial: Yr Wyddfa

Cadair Idris

Start
Minffordd

Distance
6 miles (9.5km)

Height gain
3,020 feet (920m)

Approximate time
5 hours

Route terrain
Rugged mountain upland

Parking
National Park car park (Pay and Display) at start

OS maps
Landranger 124 (Porthmadog & Dolgellau), Explorer OL23 (Cadair Idris & Llyn Tegid)

GPS waypoints
SH 732 115
Ⓐ SH 728 115
Ⓑ SH 720 123
Ⓒ SH 712 119
Ⓓ SH 711 130
Ⓔ SH 732 127
Ⓕ SH 727 120

Cadair Idris means 'Chair of Idris', Idris being a shadowy, legendary figure who allegedly inhabited the mountain. Its shapely, distinctive profile, especially its long northern face, dominates the southern region of the National Park, making it a popular and interesting climb. This route ascends and descends by the well-known Minffordd Path, which involves a lot of climbing, but rewards fit and energetic walkers with spectacular and varied terrain and extensive ever changing views.

⚠ Unless walkers are experienced in such conditions and able to use a compass, this is a walk to be avoided in bad weather, especially during the winter months, but one to be enjoyed to the full on a fine, clear day.

Take the kissing-gate by the toilet block, signed for Cadair Idris. Turn right along the wide, tree-lined track to reach a gate. Turn left in front of it and pass by Ystradllyn to reach a National Nature Reserve board beyond a stream Ⓐ.

Use the hand-gate and start a steep ascent up steps through oak woods. Beyond a wooden gate the climb soon eases; stay with the main path rising gradually left of the stream, slowly bending towards a vast amphitheatre of cliffs. At an indistinct junction beyond a fenced corner Ⓑ, turn left on a steeper path to a broken wall, then turn right. Trace this higher path, which becomes stepped and passes well to the left of a distinctive boulder with a small tree on top. It rises sharply to a low col, here bending right, now marked by frequent cairns. Down to your right is the superb glacial cwm of Llyn Cau, collared by the cliffs of the Cadair range, with Penygadair looming above.

The gradient eases for a short distance, where immense views both south and along the great ridge of Cadair to Cardigan Bay unfold, before bending right Ⓒ to climb up a steep, braided path to a ladder-stile near the summit of Craig Cau. Climb the stile and choose a way ahead across boulders, soon picking up a path down into Bwlch Cau, separating Craig Cau from Penygadair. *Use caution – there are sheer and unprotected drops on your immediate right.*

Join the wide path up from Bwlch Cau, shortly reaching the edge of the boulder field and crags that lead to the summit. The zigzag path is cairned; simply keep well away from the edge to your right to gain the trig pillar and nearby shelter on Penygadair Ⓓ.

Head east from the summit, shortly passing to the right of a sub-summit and across a small boulder field. Bear right on a distinct path across the grassy plateau towards Mynydd Moel. In a dip, fork right onto a lesser path that courses just above the break of slope high above invisible Llyn Cau. It's a clear path, marked by small cairns, heading directly for a distant wind farm. An easy scramble down a low crag leads to a boggy area, after which the path undulates amidst small crags and heathery slopes to reach a ladder-stile at a corner of fences **E**.

Climb this and turn immediately right at a waymark post. Now keep to the steep path that drops beside a fence (right). There are great views from this path down Tal-y-llyn Lake and across to the Cambrian Mountains. You'll eventually reach another ladder-stile on your right. Climb this and trace the wide path around the snout of a green knoll, dropping to a low falls on Nant Cadair **F**.

Cross here and turn left along the path, retracing this back down through the woods to the car park. ●

SCALE 1:25000 or 2½ INCHES to 1 MILE 4CM to 1KM

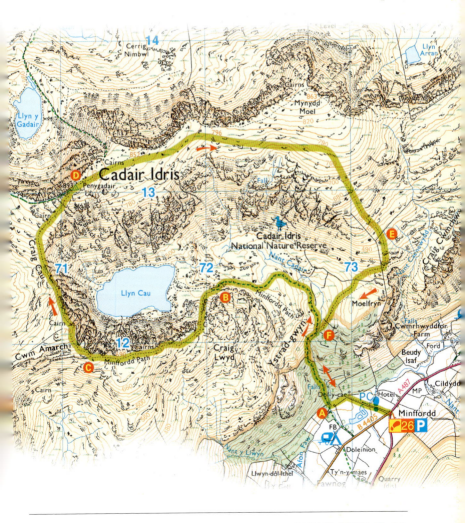

Start
Ogwen (western end of the lake)

Distance
5¼ miles (8.5km)

Height gain
2,770 feet (845m)

Approximate time
5 hours

Route terrain
Rock almost all the way; some scrambling; loose scree

Parking
At start, and lay-bys along A5

OS maps
Landranger 115 (Snowdon/Yr Wyddfa), Explorer OS OL17 (Snowdon/Yr Wyddfa)

GPS waypoints
- SH 649 604
- Ⓐ SH 661 588
- Ⓑ SH 656 583
- Ⓒ SH 642 579
- Ⓓ SH 638 585
- Ⓔ SH 646 598

Glyder Fach and Glyder Fawr

The Glyders (Glyderau in Welsh) lie between the Llanberis Pass and Nant Ffrancon, and overlook the Snowdon range to the west and the Carneddau to the east. They take their name from the twin peaks of Glyder Fach and Glyder Fawr, both of which are ascended on this walk. It is a magnificent, rugged and challenging walk amid superlative scenery, but it is also a strenuous walk suitable only for the fit and experienced mountain walker, involving some steep and energetic scrambling, and difficult descents down scree and rock.

⚠ Only attempt the walk in good summer weather, as even on a fine winter's day snow and ice near the summits make the going dangerous; it should be tackled only by walkers experienced in these conditions and properly equipped.

Start by taking the uphill, stony path at the side of the car park, by the refreshment kiosk and toilet block, continue to cross a footbridge and stick with the on-going path beyond. Where this well-constructed path bends to the right, leave it and keep ahead along a less distinct path making for Bochlwyd Buttress, a conspicuous crag ahead and to the left of a waterfall. Climb fairly steeply on the right of the falls, and at the top cross the stream on the left to continue along the left-hand side of Llyn Bochlwyd, which now appears. Go past the lake, climbing steadily to reach Bwlch Tryfan and making for a couple of ladder-stiles that span the wall there Ⓐ.

From this col, which lies between Tryfan and Glyder Fach, there is a superb view back down to Llyn Bochlwyd and the whole length of Nant Ffrancon with the Menai Strait and Anglesey beyond. Cross a stile and turn right to begin the extremely steep, often loose and quite difficult ascent of Bristly Ridge, a daunting sight. It begins by climbing to the base of the cliffs above, where a gully, not obvious from below, will appear. This is the start of the Bristly Ridge. The ascent is a challenging scramble, and previous scrambling experience will certainly help here. Most of the time the way onward is clear enough, and there are no insurmountable difficulties, but it is a form of rock climbing, and in a few places there are likely to be moments of doubt. A little casting about will locate the easiest lines, but it is impossible to give meaningful directions, except to say that near the top of the ridge the route does move a little to the right, before a final pull to the top. Overall the sensation of climbing the ridge is invigorating, and the secret to success is patience and three points of contact at all times.

Anyone having second thoughts, should opt for the steep scree route to the left of the buttress. This is a tiresome but easier option.

Whichever route you choose, once on the wide ridge turn right to find the distinctive 'Cantilever' and, beyond, the summit rocks of Glyder Fach (3,262ft/994m) **B**, which are actually quite awkward to climb on to. Continue across this increasingly surreal landscape to the pinnacles of Castell y Gwynt (Castle of the Winds). Views here are unmatched in Snowdonia, sweeping across mountain, coast, lake and moor, with the incredible

shattered rock pile as a foreground.

If you are confident scrambling, then you can find a way over the Castell y Gwynt, but there is a clear path that passes just left of the rocks, descending slightly before joining a gently rising path (always heading roughly towards the distinct peak of Snowdon). Beyond the Castell, a clear path takes you on to Glyder Fawr (3,284ft/1,001m) **C**.

From the summit, head initially in a north-westerly direction, roughly targeting the adjacent peak of Y Garn, and following a clear path through

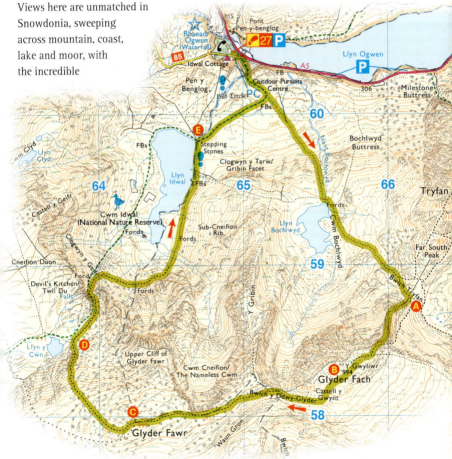

The Castle of the Winds (Castell y Gwynt), Glyder Fawr (right) and Snowdon

Glyder Fawr's boulder field. The path soon becomes very steep as it drops down a massive scree slope. Great care is needed here; your aim is to reach the right-hand side of the small lake, Llyn y Cwn **D**, to which the path leads. *But take your time and watch your footing.*

At the lake, keep right on a distinct path to reach the mouth of a gully, and there start a very testing descent, largely on roughly stepped rocks, beside the defile of The Devil's Kitchen – in Welsh 'Twll Du' (Black Hole), a very apt description of the damp, gloomy cleft in the sheer cliffs. A path leads to the base of Twll Du, should you want to take a

closer look, before continuing.

Below, your target, Llyn Idwal, gradually comes into view. And as the path becomes less steep, you'll reach an indistinct junction near a huge boulder. Keep right here to continue down to the lakeside path to the right (east) of Llyn Idwal, soon passing the rock climbing Idwal Slabs. Follow a clear path out of the cwm, to a footbridge **E** across the stream that drains the lake. Join the path that initially follows the right-hand side of this stream, remaining with this to find the junction passed early in the walk; turn left to return to the start. ●

Y Llethr and Moelfre

The Rhinogs (Rhinogydd in Welsh) have a deserved reputation for the most exasperating and trying walking conditions, and yet the highest of them, Y Llethr, is such an amazing contrast. Where the two main summits, Rhinog Fawr and Rhinog Fach, are beset with boulders, rocky outcrops and knee-deep heather, Y Llethr is almost a football pitch by comparison, a huge grassy expanse. This approach from Tal-y-bont, near Dyffryn Ardudwy is hugely agreeable, and not unduly difficult in spite of its length and height gain. The inclusion of Moelfre, a rarely visited summit, is well worthwhile, but may just as easily be omitted; not until you are making the return to Tal-y-bont do you need to decide.

From the car park at Tal-y-bont, a path leads to the **Ysgethin Inn**. Go behind this to locate a narrow path that follows the bubbling Afon Ysgethin through the pleasant woodland of Coed Cors y Gedol, a Site of Special Scientific Interest, to reach a surfaced lane near a cottage, Lletty-lloegr **A**, but not named on maps). Walk briefly to the left, to a signed path through bracken, pass to the rear of the cottage, and then follow a wall upwards through bracken and gorse to a stile in another wall bounding a wide track.

Start
Tal-y-bont, beside the Afon Ysgethin

Distance
11¾ miles (18.8km)

Height gain
2,840 feet (865m)

Approximate time
6½ hours

Route terrain
Moorland; farm tracks; woodland

Parking
Village car park at start

OS maps
Landranger 124 (Porthmadog & Dolgellau), Explorer OL18 (Harlech, Porthmadog & Bala/y Bala)

GPS waypoints
SH 589 218
A SH 606 226
B SH 639 242
C SH 660 255
D SH 622 237

MAP CONTINUES ON PAGE 90 ➡

Turn eastwards along the track, which after a couple of dog-legs, reaches open country with the rounded mound of Moelfre on your left. Stay with the on-going track, ignoring a branch that leads down to Pont Scethin (used in Walk 18). Along the way you pass below a small woodland, not far from which a scatter of ruins is all that remains of a coaching inn that served the London-Harlech stagecoach route.

As you draw level with the low point linking Moelfre with Y Llethr, an indistinct path forks left **B** and this heads up to a col on the eastern side of Moelfre.

The path improves with height and swings to the right, up to a wall that puts you on the Moelyblithcwm ridge. Follow this wall, at varying distances, as it climbs steadily towards the rounded summit of Y Llethr to the south of which it intercepts a ridge wall **C**. From here it is but a short haul to the top of Y Llethr, marked by a cairn. Views are limited from the summit; but by walking north-eastwards across the summit you will be rewarded a stunning view of Llyn Hywel and Rhinog Fach.

Llyn Hywel Renowned as the haunt of monocular fish, but since they seldom swim near the surface of the impressive lake with its tilted slabs, the truth of the assertion is difficult to pin down. Gerald of Wales (Giraldus Cambrensis), that peripatetic cleric who travelled around Wales in 1188, observed of the lake: 'It abounds in three different kinds of fish, eels, trout and perch, and all of them have only one eye, the right one being there but not the left.'

Retrace your steps across the top of Y Llethr, and drop down to the wall junction to the south. Now start to retrace your steps down the Moelyblithcwm ridge. Llyn Bodlyn, tucked in below Diffwys, is especially pleasing on the eye.

As the ground levels, so you tackle Moelfre; if you are not feeling up to it, simply miss it out and retrace your steps to the main track below. But strong walkers will have no difficulty including this minor summit, which is topped by an ancient cairn built by the people who long ago inhabited the Vale of Ardudwy at its feet.

As you ascend onto Moelfre, keep a wall on your right, and then from the summit, choose a largely untrodden line of descent beside another wall to rejoin the outward track at a gate **D**. Now retrace your steps to Tal-y-bont. ●

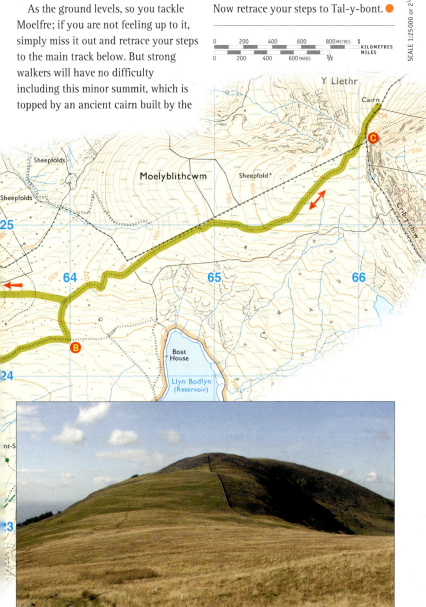

Moelfre: the line keeps left of the wall

Further Information

 ## Safety on the Hills

The hills, mountains and moorlands of Britain, though of modest height compared with those in many other countries, need to be treated with respect. Friendly and inviting in good weather, they can quickly be transformed into wet, misty, windswept and potentially dangerous areas of wilderness in bad weather. Even on an outwardly fine and settled summer day, conditions can rapidly deteriorate at high altitudes and, in winter, even more so.

Therefore it is advisable always to take both warm and waterproof clothing, sufficient nourishing food, a hot drink, first-aid kit, torch and whistle. Wear suitable footwear, such as strong walking boots or shoes that give a good grip over rocky terrain and on slippery slopes. Try to obtain a local weather forecast and bear it in mind before you start. Do not be afraid to abandon your proposed route and return to your starting point in the event of a sudden and unexpected deterioration in the weather. Do not go alone and allow enough time to finish the walk well before nightfall.

Most of the walks described in this book do not venture into remote wilderness areas and will be safe to do, given due care and respect, at any time of year in all but the most unreasonable weather. Indeed, a crisp, fine winter day often provides perfect walking conditions, with firm ground underfoot and a clarity that is not possible to achieve in the other seasons of the year. A few walks, however, are suitable only for reasonably fit and experienced hill walkers able to use a compass and should definitely not be tackled by anyone else during the winter months or in bad weather, especially high winds and mist. These are indicated in the general description that precedes each of the walks.

 ## Walkers and the Law

The Countryside and Rights of Way Act (CRoW Act 2000) extends the rights of access previously enjoyed by walkers in England and Wales. Implementation of these rights began on 19 September 2004. The Act amends existing legislation and for the first time provides access on foot to certain types of land – defined as mountain, moor, heath, down and registered common land.

Where You Can Go
Rights of Way
Prior to the introduction of the CRoW Act, walkers could only legally access the countryside along public rights of way. These are either 'footpaths' (for walkers only) or 'bridleways' (for walkers, riders on horseback and pedal cyclists). A third category called 'Byways open to all traffic' (BOATs), is used by motorised vehicles as well as those using non-mechanised transport. Mainly they are green lanes, farm and estate roads, although occasionally they will be found crossing mountainous area.

Rights of way are marked on Ordnance Survey maps. Look for the green broken lines on the Explorer maps, or the red dashed lines on Landranger maps.

The term 'right of way' means exactly what it says. It gives a right of passage over what, for the most part, is private land. Under pre-CRoW legislation walkers were required to keep to the line of the right of way and not stray onto land on either side. If you did inadvertently wander off the right of way, either because of faulty map reading or because the route was not clearly indicated on the ground, you were technically trespassing.

Local authorities have a legal obligation to ensure that rights of way are kept clear and free of obstruction, and are signposted where they leave metalled roads. The duty of local authorities to install signposts extends to the placing of signs along a path or way, but only where the authority considers it necessary to have a signpost or waymark to assist persons unfamiliar with the locality.

The New Access Rights
Access Land

As well as being able to walk on existing rights of way, under the new legislation you now have access to large areas of open land. You can of course continue to use rights of way footpaths to cross this land, but the main difference is that you can now lawfully leave the path and wander at will, but only in areas designated as access land.

Where to Walk

Areas now covered by the new access rights – Access Land – are shown on Ordnance Survey Explorer maps by a light yellow tint surrounded by a pale orange border. New orange coloured 'i' symbols on the maps will show the location of permanent access information boards installed by the access authorities.

Restrictions

The right to walk on access land may lawfully be restricted by landowners, but whatever restrictions are put into place on access land they have no effect on existing rights of way, and you can continue to walk on them.

Dogs

Dogs can be taken on access land, but must be kept on leads of two metres or less between 1 March and 31 July, and at all times where they are near livestock. In addition landowners may impose a ban on all dogs from fields where lambing takes place for up to six weeks in any year. Dogs may be banned from moorland used for grouse shooting and breeding for up to five years.

General Obstructions

Obstructions can sometimes cause a problem on a walk and the most common of these is where the path across a field has been ploughed over. It is legal for a farmer to plough up a path provided that it is restored within two weeks. This does not always happen and you are faced with the dilemma of following the line of the path, even if this means treading on crops, or walking round the edge of the field. Although the latter course of action seems the most sensible, it does mean that you would be trespassing.

Other obstructions can vary from overhanging vegetation to wire fences across the path, locked gates or even a cattle feeder on the path.

Use common sense. If you can get round the obstruction without causing damage, do so. Otherwise only remove as much of the obstruction as is necessary to secure passage.

If the right of way is blocked and cannot be followed, there is a long-standing view that in such circumstances there is a right to deviate, but this cannot wholly be relied on. Although it is accepted in law that highways (and that includes rights of way) are for the public service, and if the usual track is impassable, it is for the general good that people should be entitled to pass into another line. However, this should not be taken as indicating a right to deviate whenever a way is impassable. If in doubt, retreat.

Report obstructions to the local authority and/or the Ramblers.

 Useful Organisations

Campaign for National Parks
5-11 Lavington Street, London, SE1 0NZ
Tel. 020 7981 0890
www.cnp.org.uk

Campaign for the Protection of Rural Wales
Ty Gwyn, 31 High Street, Welshpool, Powys SY21 7YD
Tel. 01938 552525/556212
www.cprw.org.uk

Countryside Council for Wales
Maes-y-Ffynnon, Penrhosgarnedd, Bangor, Gwynedd, LL57 2DW
Tel. 0845 130 6229
www.ccw.gov.uk

Long Distance Walkers' Association
www.ldwa.org.uk

Natural Resources Wales
Tel. 0300 065 3000
Bangor office
Maes y Ffynnon, Penrhosgarnedd,
Bangor, LL57 2DW
Dolgellau office
Government Buildings, Arran Road,
Dolgellau, LL40 1LW
www.naturalresources.wales

National Trust
Membership and general enquiries:
Tel. 0344 800 1895
Wales regional office
Priest House, Tredegar House,
Newport, NP10 8YW
Tel. 01633 811659
www.nationaltrust.org.uk

North Wales Tourism
www.gonorthwales.co.uk

Ordnance Survey
Tel. 03456 05 05 05 (Lo-call)
www.ordnancesurvey.co.uk

Ramblers' Wales
3 Coopers Yard, Curran Road,
Cardiff CF10 5NB
Tel. 029 2064 4308
www.ramblers.org.uk/wales

Snowdonia National Park Authority
National Park Office,
Penrhyndeudraeth,
Gwynedd LL48 6LF
Tel. 01766 770274
www.eryri.npa.gov.uk

National Park Information Centres:
Aberdyfi: 01654 767321
Beddgelert: 01766 890615
Betws-y-Coed: 01690 710426

Snowdonia Society
Caban, Brynrefail, Caernarfon,
Gwynedd LL55 3NR
Tel. 01286 685498
www.snowdonia-society.org.uk

Tourist Information
Visit Snowdonia
www.visitsnowdonia.info

Local Tourist Information Centres:
Bala: 01341 280787
Betws-y-Coed: 01690 710426
Caernarfon: 01286 672232
Conwy: 01492 592248
Dolgellau: 01341 422888
Llandudno: 01492 577577
Porthmadog: 01766 512981

Youth Hostels Association
Trevelyan House, Dimple Road,
Matlock DE4 3YH
Tel. 01629 592700 (reservations)
www.yha.org.uk

 Ordnance Survey maps for Snowdonia

This area is covered by Ordnance Survey 1:50 000 (1¼ inches to 1 mile or 2cm to 1km) scale Landranger map sheets 115, 116, 124 and 125. These all purpose maps are packed with information to help you explore the area. Viewpoints, picnic sites, places of interest and caravan and camping sites are shown, as well as public rights of way information such as footpaths and bridleways. To examine Snowdonia in more detail, and especially if you are planning walks, Ordnance Survey Explorer maps:

OL17 (Snowdon / Yr Wyddfa)
OL18 (Harlech, Porthmadog & Bala/y Bala)
OL23 (Cadair Idris & Llyn Tegid)
all at 1:25 000 (2½ inches to1 mile or 4cm to 1km) scale are ideal.

Text: Terry Marsh
Photography: Terry Marsh and p17, Jon Young
Editorial: Ark Creative (UK) Ltd
Design: Ark Creative (UK) Ltd

ISBN: 978-0-319-09014-5

While every care has been taken to ensure the accuracy of the route directions, the
publishers cannot accept responsibility for errors or omissions, or for changes in
details given. The countryside is not static: hedges and fences can be removed, field
boundaries can alter, stiles can be replaced by gates, footpaths can be rerouted and
changes in ownership can result in the closure or diversion of some concessionary
paths. Also, paths that are easy and pleasant for walking in fine conditions may
become slippery, muddy and difficult in wet weather, while stepping stones across
rivers and streams may become impassable.

   If you find an inaccuracy in either the text or maps, please write to Crimson
Publishing at the address below.

First published 1991 by Jarrold Publishing.
Revised and reprinted 1993, 1995, 1996, 1998, 2002, 2004, 2006, 2008, 2010.

This edition first published in Great Britain 2012 by Crimson Publishing and reprinted
with amendments in 2016 and 2017.

Crimson Publishing, 19-21C Charles Street, Bath, BA1 1HX

www.pathfinderwalks.co.uk

Printed in India by Replika Press Pvt. Ltd. 14/17

A catalogue record for this book is available from the British Library.

Front cover: Pen yr Ole Wen and Llyn Idwal
Page 1: Tryfan from Bristly Ridge

Ordnance Survey

Pathfinder® Guides

Britain's best-loved walking guides